The Role of Assessment in Schools

The Role of Assessment in Schools

A new edition of
The Role of Testing in Schools

Ray Sumner

NFER-NELSON

Published by The NFER-NELSON Publishing Company Ltd,
Darville House, 2 Oxford Road East,
Windsor, Berkshire SL4 1DF, England

First Published, 1987
Revised Edition, 1991
© 1991, Ray Sumner

The moral rights of the author have been asserted.

British Library Cataloguing in Publication Data
Sumner, R. (Raymond), 1929–
    The role of assessment in schools.–New ed.
    1. Schools. Students. Assessment
    I. Title
    371.264

    ISBN 0–7005–1263–2

Phototypeset by Input Typesetting Ltd, London
Printed by Billing & Sons Ltd, Worcester

ISBN 0–7005–1263–2
Code 8263–02–1

Contents

List of Figures and Tables

Preface and Acknowledgements

In the two years since the first version of this book was written, the government's intentions to test pupils at certain stages in schooling have been turned into detailed plans. The scheme is limited in that it applies only to attainments prescribed by the National Curriculum. Though it naturally dominates the current discussion of assessment, it would be a mistake to neglect other aspects of pupils' development and other forms of testing. Though contexts particularly, and techniques, may change, the principles are much the same. Hence, much of the original text remains unaltered, but there are substantial additions and amendments mainly intended to address the national testing and assessment proposals.

Only a few tests are mentioned specifically, usually because their features are relevant to the topic under discussion. In these cases attribution is pertinent and fair to the originators. Those tests which are identified were chosen as illustrative examples rather than necessarily commendable ones. Indeed, test reviews over the years in the USA and more recently in the UK have tended not to commend tests, mainly because of technical inadequacies or the lack of data in manuals about the valid applications of pupils' results.

There are, however, encouraging signs that tests are beginning to meet the criteria which discerning users rightly expect. In turn, the user needs appropriate knowledge and skills, especially those necessary to choosing tests aptly, administering them correctly and evaluating the results analytically.

Expertise in testing is a small part of the expertise required for skilled teaching. Because certain aspects of tests and their uses are complex, in some schools there may be a place for a specialist who can guide policy and assist colleagues when implementing testing.

A most valuable role that a teacher might take is one of critical consumer; one who will question authors and publishers, so that the quality of the materials available to schools will continue to rise.

I wish to thank Lynne McFarland for promoting the work and the critical reviewers who drew attention to many aspects which could be improved. Despite their good advice, deficiencies remain, for which I take responsibility. I wish to thank Wendy Crees, most particularly for her patient and skilled word processing and drawing, which transformed a series of drafts into a readable typescript. Also, I am indebted to Roda Morrison and Carolyn Richardson for their expert editorial contribution and to Tim Cornford for his advice in incorporating the recent additions in the text.

Ray Sumner
January 1990

Introduction

This book has two main aims: the first is to enable teachers to use educational tests with insight; the second is to provide the basic knowledge with which teachers can become critical consumers in a rapidly expanding market place. Both of these aims entail focusing on the aims of testing and test results, but with a good understanding of how the two are related. In this context it is possible to appreciate the advantages and limitations of different kinds of test, and to judge whether a particular test is likely to meet the educational purpose which is envisaged by prospective users.

Because the recent UK legislation on the National Curriculum and the requirements to assess pupils at the end of certain 'key stages' (more fully described on pages 2 to 4), it is relevant to consider 'what is a test?' and 'what is an assessment?'. Briefly, a test consists of a task or series of tasks given to a pupil according to a prescribed procedure; the pupil's response is subjected to a scoring or a classificatory procedure by an assessor (or someone following an assessor's directions); this direct observation then forms the basis for making an inference about the pupil, usually in respect of a particular attribute. Whilst a test is one form of assessment, other forms utilize procedures which do not include a task-response sequence. For example, observing pupils at work, questioning or conversing with them or looking at samples of their work can all provide information to an assessor leading to inferences about particular attributes. Both tests and other types of assessments can give pupils (and others with a legitimate concern) insight about themselves when there is appropriate feedback.

The term 'test' is used extensively throughout this book to refer to a very broad range of materials and procedures, which fall within the definition given above. The government's proposals for assessing pupils' progress in the National Curriculum were initially referred to as tests but more latterly they are presented generically as assessments. In fact, the system being set up will have two parts, as follows: (a) centrally prescribed tests (called Standard Assessment Tasks or SATs) and (b) teachers' assessments (some of which may indeed be tests, as defined above) which may be moderated, that is, modified, through procedures utilizing the latest (SAT) results as a basis for inter-teacher and inter-school judgements. There is much in sound tests and testing procedures that can be paralleled in other forms of assessment. It therefore behoves teachers, who will all be involved in assessments made for records of achievement and National Curriculum assessments, to become more fully informed about tests and testing.

Like teaching, testing should be purposeful; and when a test is used, it should be the most suitable of the various forms of assessment which might be available. A large range of purposes can be defined. Some of these relate closely to work done with pupils, others concern the curriculum, the organization of schools or education authority procedures. Regrettably, as inquiries have shown (Gipps *et al.*, 1983), teachers either have been uncertain about their reasons for using tests or have administered them routinely at someone else's behest. Whilst there are reasonably legitimate circumstances, such as national surveys of attainment when testing may be done on behalf of a remote third party, for the most part those who do the testing should be aware of its objects and of the bases for the tests they administer. They will then be in a position to collaborate helpfully in the procedure or, if need be, to criticize sensibly what is going on.

In the UK there are currently being published more tests than ever before, and more tests are being given to pupils than in previous eras. Indeed, the government has used this circumstance as a justification for the testing programme it will require teachers to carry out in parallel with the National Curriculum, being introduced from 1989 onwards. In this setting the claims made by test authors or those responsible for testing programmes deserve especially critical examination because any failure to meet them involves a waste of pupils' time, teaching effort and resources which could have been used for some other purpose.

Tests have undoubtedly acquired a mystique of their own, possibly because training courses have given assessment scant attention; and maybe the aura of external examinations has reflected an opaque prestige too. The statistical basis for tests, as revealed in the manuals and tables for transforming scores, also tends to mark out the field as one for the specialist rather than being accessible to all. Tests and testing are indeed complex in many respects, but no more so than other aspects of school education. A further, crucial point is that computers will carry out the processing of results much more efficiently than people; so test users nowadays need to understand analytical concepts rather than learn statistical techniques.

One concept which tends to be forgotten when technicalities abound and jargon multiplies is that because testing ought to be purposeful there are 'clients'. These are the constituents of the education service whose needs are its reason for being. Some of these client bodies are readily identified. At various times, in the author's experience, these have been: education committee members; LEA officers and advisers; the HMI; careers officers; the DES; educational psychologists; parents; and headteachers and teachers. Then there is that large, amorphous body of clients – the pupils – who should directly or indirectly benefit from the *results* of testing.

However, for test results to be of any benefit they have to be interpreted or applied in a valid fashion. At one time, a frequently quoted definition of test validity was 'a test is valid if it tests what it purports to test'. This definition is not acceptable these days as it is recognized (in standards formulated in North America and the UK, referred to later) that a test is valid only if the results can be applied effectively to some specified purpose. The emphasis on application directs our attention closely to the needs of the clients, and especially to relevant educational goals.

Of course, 'what schools are for' is continually being redefined through the expectations articulated by society in dialogue with professional educationists. In England and Wales, legislation enacted in 1988 (the Education Reform Act) will ensure that the great majority of schools will teach a common curriculum, defined by pupil attainment targets and programmes of study. Also, schools will take part in a national testing programme which will yield assessments for each pupil in the system at the ages of 7, 11, 14 and 16 years. Much of the impetus towards adaptation has arisen formally through the agency of various government committees, recruited to review problematic areas of education and recommend ways of improving them. These national inquiries have all raised assessments as issues relevant to progress. Their recommendations have fundamentally changed the notion of what teachers ought to be competent to do.

This book takes as its starting-point the background of changing outlooks on education together with the growing demands on schools, particularly in regard to assessment. The features of tests and the purposes that they serve are then analysed as a framework for consideration of what tests can measure. Next the wide variety of matters which test constructors may regard as options are described in relation to the generally accepted categories of tests.

One feature many tests have in common, which usually confuses teachers, is the treatment of test scores, particularly their transformation into other kinds of scale. Accordingly, the bases for several kinds of scale are clarified, and a case is made for dropping certain outmoded practices (that is, reading age and attainment quotients). Then because test scores can rarely be interpreted or applied without reference to other data, a number of statistical concepts (and terms) are elucidated which enable scores to be evaluated or used to inform decisions.

The final chapters focus on the interpretation of test results, the circumstances which may affect pupils' performance and (because they add depth to an interpretation) the concepts and techniques which are commonly employed in test construction and other forms of assessment. Teachers should find here much that can be used to improve the preparation of their own test materials, also its use in relation to pupils' learning and the curriculum.

Throughout the book it is stressed that testing should never become an end in itself. Nor should the results be accepted blindly as they form only one source of information upon which to base professional judgements.

CHAPTER 1
The Increasing Involvement of Teachers in the Assessment of Pupils

The educational climate

There is no need to dwell on the ways in which the educational climate in the UK has changed so markedly over recent years. The move towards comprehensive schooling and raising of the statutory leaving age to 16 in the late 1960s undoubtedly sparked off public debate about school organization and the curriculum which, until recently, has overshadowed the more private concerns of parents about the quality of schooling received by their children. The decline of selection to grammar schools at age 11, which currently affects about 12 per cent of pupils of this age in England and Wales across 33 LEAs, tended to shift the emphasis at the primary school stage from differentiation into groups towards developing each child as an individual. At the secondary stage the growing influence of external examinations reinforced the belief that children ought to get something tangible out of their school experience.

In the 1980s, central government has added its weight to the movement to change LEAs and schools through the acquisition of wide-ranging powers. These include:

- legislation giving parents better access to procedures for appealing against the allocation of their child to a particular school;
- extending the responsibilities of school governors to include the curriculum;
- altering the composition of the governing body to include

more parents and promoting the concept of accountability to the community in which schools are located;
- introducing a national curriculum and pupil testing;
- delegating finance and management to the majority of schools.

Previously, a string of committees (Bullock, 1975; Taylor, 1977; Warnock, 1978; Cockcroft, 1982; Swann, 1985) inquired into areas of major importance and produced recommendations aimed at improving standards of attainment. Assessment figures quite prominently in the committees' recommendations, which LEAs and teacher education establishments read as agendas for in-service staff development. From the standpoint of testing, the 1988 Education Reform Act is unique in that the law requires pupils to be tested towards the end of 'key stages' in school education.

Whilst the provisions of the National Curriculum have gained wide acceptance, the proposals for testing remain controversial. Their origins might be traced variously to practice in several States in the USA, to graded tests of proficiency in modern languages, to graded assessments of stage by stage courses in Mathematics, Science, and CDT, developed by the London and East Anglia Examination Board and teams at Chelsea College, University of London; and more remotely, to the graded Music examinations and the motor vehicle driving test. The prevailing notion is that each child should develop to his or her full extent; a desire to which teachers naturally subscribe. Each pupil's progress will have to be assessed, as a matter of sound pedagogical practice. The National Curriculum makes it possible to have national tests, which lead towards the integration of teaching and assessment as an aid for learning.

The scheme was worked out during the passage of the 1988 Education Reform Act through parliament. A small task group, called the Task Group on Assessment and Testing (TGAT), worked to a brief sent to them by the Secretary of State for Education, Mr Baker. Their report (DES and Welsh Office, 1988) supported the most contentious of the Act's proposals, that is, to test pupils at or near the age of 7 years; and formulated a system for testing pupils at or near the ages of 7, 11, 14 and 16 years. Its essence was that assessments would consist of tests or tasks; these could be matched with programmes of study in certain 'core' and 'foundation' subjects in the curriculum, each embodying sets of 'attainment targets' for each age-group; a ten-point scale would differentiate attainment over the five to 16 age range; and the subjects would each be specified by components comprised of attainment target sets.

The group gave priority to the need 'to show what a pupil has learned and mastered'. The purposes of the system were defined as (i) *formative* at the 7, 11 and 14 year ages, that is, the information helps with the next stage in learning, (ii) *diagnostic* or indicative of the need for diagnostic assessment, that is, appraising an individual pupil's learning difficulties, (iii) *summative* at the age of 16, that is, showing attainments achieved by that stage, and (iv) *evaluative*, that is, class, year-groups, school and LEA summaries of results would be prepared and used to examine progress in terms of the National Curriculum. Results would be reported to the interested parties in the following way. Each pupil's parents must receive a profile of their child's performance. Except for the seven-year-olds, aggregated results for classes, schools and LEAs must be produced. Those for LEAs must be accompanied by a general statement about the area indicating 'the nature of socio-economic and other influences which are known to affect schools'. Aggregated results for the seven-year-old groups in a school may be published, but this is discretionary. Prior to administering the national tests, called Standard Assessment Tasks (SATs), teachers will make their own assessments of each pupil (Teachers' Assessments, TAs). The TGAT also proposed that the assessments obtained from both sources, the SATs and TAs, would be standardized for each age-group by a process of moderation, which would involve all of the teachers taking a part in testing their pupils. The basic idea of moderation (described more fully in the Postscript, p. 215) is that when parts of the national tests or tasks have to be judged as to scale level by teachers, the variations bound to occur because of differing interpretations of criteria and performance can be brought onto a common standard, that is, the variations will be moderated (or alternatively, the tasks will be calibrated). The TGAT were very committed to this aspect of teacher involvement, seeing it as essential for gaining understanding of progress in relation to programmes of study in curriculum areas, but the government's initial response was not enthusiastic (too expensive, complicates assessment process, undue influence given to teachers). Subsequently, the Schools Assessment and Examination Council (SEAC) in 1989 recommended to the Secretary of State for Education and Science that the SAT results would supplant teachers' assessments (Halsey, 1989). Whereas the original scheme envisaged testing pupils in all attainment targets, the SEAC recommendation foresaw that some would not be assessed by the use of SATs. The TGAT members had declared their commitment to involving teachers closely in moderating the final assessment by examining SAT results alongside their own. Three of their number reacted to the recommendation to give SAT results precedence by publicly criticizing the move as one likely to diminish the value of the teachers' own assessments (Allanson, 1989).

The report makes it clear that assessing pupils at other ages is highly desirable, especially when it is aimed at diagnosing individual learning problems. It does not rule out LEA schemes or other schemes schools might have, though it draws some justification for a national system from the multiplicity of testing in schools and LEAs, which shows little consistency as a whole. Secondary teachers will recognize the model adopted by the TGAT as similar to the 16 plus examinations, which combine externally prescribed tests or tasks with internally made teachers' assessments (using guides to criteria and procedures). With the emphasis given to progress on the National Curriculum and periodic national tests, it seems unlikely that examinations at 16 plus will remain unchanged for the core and foundation subjects; that is, English, Mathematics, Science and Technology, History, Geography, Art, Music, Physical Education and a Modern Foreign Language. For example, these examinations could be rationalized by reducing the total number of different papers produced by the examinations board and broadening the range to accommodate the so-called lower ability pupils.

The implications of implementing the TGAT system in full are manifold, and many are dealt with in later chapters. These include training for teachers in administering tests or tasks and training in making assessments in line with the scale levels according to the matching criteria. In secondary schools, most subject specialist teachers will see this as a sweeping modification to suit a particular system, as compared with the free choice available through the syllabuses and examinations they have had traditionally. The impact will be on schools and classroom organization for testing the 14-year-olds, and on teachers' time for marking, moderation and reporting.

School systems are bound to change, too, as the phasing of reports to parents and governors will follow on from the testing and data analysis activities. In primary schools, where few teachers specialize, apart from training in the national programmes of study, training in assessing a whole class in several 'subjects' will be needed. Though a task given to pupils may embody several 'components' (as described in Chapter 3) in more than one subject, the process of assessment will be extremely complex; and it will require managing within the everyday learning/teaching context. Indeed, because attempts were being made to produce SATs which incorporate normal classroom learning features, there was some optimism that the six- and seven-year-old pupils may not even realize they were being tested (Halsey interviewed by Nash, 1989).

Perhaps the most far-reaching implications of the 1988 legislation bear more upon teachers' relations with the pupils' parents and the local community, because they can manage within the school how they adapt teaching methods to accommodate the National Curriculum and assessment. The aspect that is less amenable is the public disclosure of assessment results. The comparisons between schools, the LEA and the national norms will be regarded as hot news. Headteachers and governors need to be aware that well-presented information which interprets and highlights pupils' attainments can help elected members and journalists to appreciate the extent to which pupils have achieved particular standards. They should translate the distributions (percentages of pupils assigned to each scale level) on profile components into descriptions of proficiencies or capabilities, and ought also to discourage crude statistical-type simplifications (for example, averaging all component levels as if they are scores), by illustrating how misleading these methods can be.

The condensed version of the TGAT report issued to schools (1988) said that there was no place in the system recommended for norm-referenced testing (see definitions in Chapter 4). It is true that in a lock-step system of teaching the only criteria taken into account should be those which demonstrate proficiency in terms of the attainment target programme of study for a given level. However, schools may wish to continue with practices which they have found to be helpful. Such practices may be operated parallel to or in conjunction with the TGAT testing system. In the short run, however, the imperatives of teaching the National Curriculum and the workload entailed by the TGAT scheme may combine to exclude other types of testing. This would be a pity, as many effective procedures have been devised, to the benefit of countless numbers of pupils.

Furthermore, the provisions of the 1981 Education Act still apply. The Act epitomizes the trend towards meeting the educational needs of individual pupils. Special education, it is said, should occur for children with significantly greater difficulty in learning than the majority of children of the same age, or disability which hinders use of the facilities generally provided. Government advice (DES Circular 1/83) on the interpretation of the legislation distinguished between 'Assessment in Schools' and 'Formal Statutory Procedures'. Arrangements in schools should allow for the progressive involvement of professionals from the class teacher to the head, a specialist teacher, an educational psychologist and the school doctor, with access to others in the health, social and educational services. It was noted that the teacher occupies 'a key position' to observe pupils' responses and identify the child experiencing learning difficulties, and to help meet the child's needs through various approaches. For a small proportion of children whose needs might be such as to require special educational provision formal assessment procedures can be implemented after the LEA has notified parents of its intentions. Thereafter, a 'multi-professional assessment' (MPA) is required (with at least a psychologist and doctor, but with others as relevant) which leads to a 'Statement'. The primary object of the Statement is the specification of what will be done to help the child cope in educational terms, though the nature of the special provision might well be physical.

The Warnock Report (1978) envisaged that as many as 20 per cent of pupils at some time in their school careers would have learning difficulty, as defined above. For some pupils their learning problems might be only temporary, whereas for others they would change, or persist; hence all pupils identified have to be reviewed periodically. No proportion was estimated for the pupils who would require Statements. In some respects this would be dependent on the special arrangements an LEA could make, as compared with educating children in ordinary schools without additional specialist resources. From the standpoint of teachers it is instructive to know what kinds of information could be called for. The list given in Circular 1/83 includes physical and emotional states, cognitive functioning, communication skills (verbal comprehension, expressive language, speech), perceptual and motor skills, adaptive skills, social skills and interaction, attitudes to learning, educational attainments, self-image, interests and behaviour. The most well-known feature of the 1981 Act is the move away from segregating different categories of handicapped pupils into separate schools or units as far as reasonably can be achieved. A less well-known aspect is that the concept of special needs should be applied to all children including the intellectually able and gifted. (A booklet by Welton, Wedell and Vorhaus, 1982, provides an excellent review of the 1981 Act implications.)

The Act has the effect of involving teachers of all kinds in the identification of pupils and the planning of provision with regard to special needs. The 1988 Education Reform Act reinforces this position through the expectation that the National Curriculum assessment procedures will lead to the identification of the learning difficulties of pupils who do not reach the attainment targets associated with particular ages; thereafter, diagnostic testing or other kinds of assessments will point the way towards promoting further learning. The 1988 Act requires that schools have to make a case to 'disapply' the National Curriculum only in the aspects which are warranted by a pupil's particular learning difficulties. Quite obviously the teacher is seen as the person in the best position to prompt action, and this has to be based upon assessments of the attributes noted above, together with appropriate records. There is thus an obligation on all teachers to have available reasonably accurate and relevant information upon which to base decisions about children's access to appropriate forms of educational experience. In this context different types of appropriate test results can be an important source of information.

Primary schools have not had the same attention accorded to them as secondary schools in recent years, but there have been pronounced changes in that sector too. One trend has been towards more active parental involvement with school-work; another has been renewed emphasis given to 'the basic skills', though the school inspectorate has stressed the value of a balanced curriculum which includes science, physical activities, technology and the arts, suggestions now given the weight of law in the National Curriculum legislation. The tension inhering in this situation was evident in LEAs where various age-groups of children (that is, in particular school years) were tested in Reading and Mathematics to gauge how far individual schools, or the LEA as a whole, measured up to or surpassed 'average' performance in the basic curriculum. Yet at the same time, LEAs attempted to promote a wider balance in the curriculum through in-service training.

The previous sections show that teachers are expected to be competent at a growing range of tasks, many of them in the fields of assessment and record keeping. In the context of teaching and learning a curriculum a great deal could be done by drawing up work plans which have assessments as an integral part of *the course* (Engel-Clough, Davies and Sumner, 1984). Doing so entails abandoning many of the routines practised in schools, such as weekly homework or periodic examinations, and replacing them by assessments which serve an educational purpose aligned closely to the objectives of course parts. In other contexts, such as the transfer of pupils from schools in one phase to the next, standardized assessments including tests have a value. Their use might embrace placing pupils into teaching groups, identifying children who may have learning difficulties and planning appropriate curricula.

Changes of the kind described carry the inference that teachers' skills should be developed accordingly. They also imply that more tests which relate closely to children's learning are required. These would give immediate information which could aid teaching and also provide helpful background for discussions with parents or colleagues, especially for children with learning problems.

Perhaps the most pressing requirement where teachers are concerned is the know-how to decide whether or not tests can be used effectively in school and classroom situations. A supposition here is that the problems pupils encounter and the decisions inhering in their amelioration are fully appreciated. The question then becomes: how can assessment results be obtained and interpreted, so that the right decisions can be made? The situations are legion but in certain problem areas there are few suitable established tests, whilst in others there is a plethora. The difficulty for the practitioner is that employing a test effectively depends upon knowledge of test characteristics and, in some cases, competence in applying certain techniques. Another pertinent issue is, in comparison with the other kinds of assessment which could be used, why use a test?

CHAPTER 2
Tests as Educational Assessments

Assessment bases

The reasons for using tests are bound up with the nature of the information they yield; and this depends entirely on the features built into a test. One justification which is frequently given is that tests are 'objective', and so free of the biases that can affect other forms of assessment. On its own, however, this reason is not sufficient. Also, as we shall see, objectivity is a matter of some debate. What really matters is whether or not a test produces good quality information. In beginning to think about quality we need to ask fundamental questions, such as: who is being assessed; who are the assessors; what do we know about the attributes assessed and how are they defined for testing?

Amongst the many types of educational assessments, tests are the most formalized. At the other extreme are the idiosyncratic impressions gained by a visitor from a short spell in a classroom talking with children. Both of these are information gathering techniques which can suit particular circumstances very well. In the case of tests the questions asked are presented to all pupils, in the same format, with the same instructions and under similar conditions. There are several less well-known differences too. For tests (when properly constructed) the questions have been chosen to reflect a characteristic which is found in the population of pupils under consideration. In contrast, when a visitor questions a pupil, the first reply and the manner in which it is given affect the subsequent question, and so on. To some extent, the line followed by the questioner depends upon which pupils are chosen as the representatives of the class. These instances bring out the importance of three populations; these are (1) the population of pupils, (2) the population of assessors and (3) the population of questions which could be formulated.

Populations of pupils are readily characterized. In national surveys, all the pupils in a particular school year might be the population of interest. In an authority different populations may be of concern; examples are:

- all children attending nursery units;
- all pupils not entered for any external examination;
- all pupils attending mathematics enrichment sessions;
- the body of students enrolled at FE and tertiary colleges.

Other populations can easily be defined. In a school the various populations might be:

- everyone on the register on 1 September;
- the pupils in a single class or set;
- all of the children who cannot swim, etc.

It is obvious that schools could identify individuals in certain populations with little difficulty, whereas LEAs would have to take considerable trouble – and to do so nationally might be impossible. In defining populations firm criteria are essential (for example, the population of pupils who have received a special needs Statement; cf. all those pupils who are 'good' at chess). In principle, however, all of the individuals in populations consisting of people can be identified and counted.

The national populations of assessors are fairly well known in the educational world; these are:

- all members of Her Majesty's Inspectorate of Schools;
- all of the examiners paid by the external examining bodies;
- the staff of the DES Assessment of Performance Unit (APU) and all of the APU survey teams (for English,

Modern Languages, Science, Mathematics, Design and Technology);

- the National Curriculum attainment target test constructors and those who administer the tests and moderate them;
- all the teachers assessing pupils using National Curriculum guidelines and criteria.

More locally, populations might be identified as:

- an LEA's inspectorate or its advisers;
- all of the teachers or lecturers in an LEA's employ;
- the body of educational psychologists;
- all of the careers advisers.

And a couple of sub-populations, for instance, might be all of the teachers involved in a graded modern languages scheme, and secondly, the teachers in a single primary school who teach the seven- to eight-year-old classes. (Problem: does this include the headteacher who takes each teacher's class for a period a week while the teacher prepares science apparatus?) Despite queries of this kind, in principle every member of these populations can be identified. What is less certain is that common assessment criteria are applied by every member of an assessor population. In fact obtaining agreement amongst even compact sets of assessors can be a major problem.

The third type of population, of questions, is not easily specified. Some example definitions are:

- all questions about science appropriate to pupils aged 13 years (the APU Science survey teams had a Science Activity Categories framework for this domain);
- all the pre-reading tasks that children aged three and four might be asked to perform;
- every possible integrated assessment task that can be devised for a specified level of a given National Curriculum attainment target;
- every pair of whole number sums in the range 1 to 5, that is, $1 + 1, 1 + 2, 1 + 3, 1 + 4, 1 + 5, 2 + 2, 2 + 3, 2 + 4, 2 + 5, 3 + 3, 3 + 4, 3 + 5, 4 + 4, 4 + 5$ and $5 + 5$.

The last population is fully specified, whereas the first three are highly dependent on concepts which may not be held universally, that is, what is appropriate science education for 13-year-olds? What are pre-reading skills, if they exist? What are apt contexts for learning or performing an attainment target?

When a teacher designs a test for a class, the course syllabus constitutes the reference frame, but the material covered by the class as it has been taught is likely to be the domain *actually* used as the basis for questions. In this situation the teacher has control over all of the judgements entailed. When the population of pupils is less restricted (for example, all of the pupils in a year group) and there are more members of the assessor population, control over judgements occurs in various ways, sometimes by consensus or alternatively through the authority of a chief examiner or area moderator.

In classroom situations it is clearly essential that teachers obtain evidence about the learning achieved by their pupils. Much of this feedback can be obtained from the transactions between teachers and pupil, and from the teacher's obser-vations of what the pupils are doing, scrutiny of their work, and so on. Comparability between teachers is not an issue; what counts is the teacher's skill in creating judgement situ-ations and sensitivity in using the information (see Harris and Bell, 1986, for a clear synthesis of theory and practice with helpful annotated references). Taking an extreme view of the individualized teaching situation, each *teacher* is unique (does not belong to a population), his/her *domain* is unique (no one else could ask the same questions of their pupils) and the *class* is unique (its characteristics are not shared by any other group of children).

More realistically, teachers and pupils face a variety of situ-ations which entail a corresponding range of roles. In the close-up tutoring role there is uniqueness, whilst in many other roles the situation demands comparability. For instance, a teacher preparing a class for a fifth-year external examination joins in a sense the sub-population of teachers of the same subject involved in the same enterprise, as do the pupils. The domain for their endeavours is specified by the syllabus and this, in turn, specifies in general terms the population of questions which could be asked. The problem shared by all of the teachers and pupils is that they do not know what *sample* of questions will be asked. In fact the technical problem facing the examiners is that, to be consistent, every year's *sample of questions* should represent the population of questions (which should reflect the domain of skills and knowledge embodied in the course).

The problem of consistency is compounded by having a large body of examiners (another sub-population), any one of whom could receive any parcel of scripts (a sub-sample from the population of answers generated by the examinees). The variability in judging answers which is inherent in the population is controlled, to some extent, by issuing examiners with guidelines or mark schemes and by chief examiners spotting for aberrant individual examiners, then modifying their results.

Compared with external school examinations, tests have a more limited scope in several ways. Usually they are for a particular age range or type of pupil and are aimed at producing information restricted to a confined domain. It is frequently asserted that tests provide objective information as distinct from the subjective information which is obtained from observations, conversations, essays or appraisal of work pieces. Only in one respect is this true: when, in tests, judgements about what counts as a correct answer are fully specified. However, test constructors' judgements about what constitutes a domain (for example, reading questions and answers for a test for six-year-olds) can only be regarded as objective *if justified* in the light of knowledge of the domain, otherwise the judgements would be subjective in the absence of a rational case. Objectivity, then, is about public disclosure and informed deliberation, in contrast to private, intuitive judgements (which may be extremely valuable). The rightful place of tests in a set of assessment tools has to be justified not on grounds of objectivity, but on account of aptness for purpose.

The preceding discussion of populations has shown that, typically, there is variation between individual members (the peas in a pod are not identical). Also that on occasions the variation is such that it is helpful to think in terms of sub-populations. These tend to be more homogeneous and also to have particular requirements. We have also seen that teachers accept different roles according to circumstances (which sometimes are not of their own choosing). Under these conditions there are probably a majority of occasions when teachers' own judgements will be entirely appropriate, and a minority when some other reference point will be desirable. A further aspect which has been touched upon is consistency of judgements or comparability between judges; in other words, the reliability of the information upon which to base decisions. Examples of circumstances when information from testing can either supplement teachers' professional judgements or produce useful information independently of teachers are now considered.

Testing purposes

Some of the purposes for which test results can be used have been mentioned already. However, a more systematic discussion is called for which will highlight the kinds of decision which would be informed through knowledge of pupils' performance at tests. A most important point which tends to be assumed rather than thought out is that testing, like any other form of assessment, should be done to enable educational policies to be carried out. Assessment practices are frequently confused with policies. For example, there are several facets to the 'policy' that every pupil should be given a compulsory homework, which will be marked, in every timetabled subject once a week. This is justified more often than otherwise on the grounds that parents can then question their children about having no homework to do when that happens. No doubt, the educational policy behind setting regular homework is that the pupil is encouraged to develop self-motivated work habits and to cover the curriculum more thoroughly than lessons would allow. In line with this learning intention marking homework, or testing pupils on it, is intended to indicate progress. Summing the homework marks gives a global index of progress made over a period of time.

  Brief reflection on the homework case shows that a number of assumptions need to be examined to decide whether the policy of indicating to the pupil, teachers and parents the amount of overall progress made by a pupil is being achieved.

Perhaps the most crucial question is: 'what do the marks awarded really show?' Do they indicate the amount of learning achieved or do they reflect other differences between pupils? In the discussion of testing goals which follows assumptions of this kind are mentioned, but more technical points are not discussed as these are dealt with later on.

Policies external to the school

For the most part, these policies originate in LEAs with two notable exceptions, that is, National Curriculum attainment target assessments and the testing undertaken as part of the national surveys of pupil performance on behalf of the APU. These have been reported at length (in HMSO publications) and the Unit has issued booklets describing assessment frameworks and results from tests of interest to teachers (of Mathematics, English, Modern Languages and Science, and Design Technology). Because the national monitoring survey testing has been described so fully elsewhere, the methods are not described here though some reference is made to certain features and innovations. Attainment target assessments are considered later though at the time of writing (1989) only some features can be identified with certainty. The Schools Examination and Assessment Council interpreted the TGAT's recommendations through the invitations it issued to various organizations to tender for the test development work for two age-groups of pupils. Though different approaches to devising the Standard Assessment Tasks (SATs) were commissioned, the Council very commendably left itself room to choose the tasks and associated methods that promise to be the most feasible and acceptable.

Transfer information
Many LEA record schemes include provision for test results; these can be entered on transfer documents together with other information about the child (disabilities, ethnic origin, outstanding talents, progress in published schemes, and so on). The broad policy, which is implied rather than spelt out, is that the pupil's transition from one school to the next will

be helped. How this goal is implemented depends on the decisions made by the school which receives the pupils. Some schools use ability test scores (for verbal, symbolic, possibly spatial reasoning) to place pupils in streams or bands; others use the same information to create classes of 'mixed-ability' children of roughly equivalent composition. (An extended discussion of practices and proposals for improvement is given by Sumner, 1986.)

Results from attainment test scores can be used in altogether different ways: to tell a subsequent teacher about the pupils' knowledge and skills, usually in Mathematics and English; to inform class teachers about the standards achieved by the group they will teach; to gauge the attainment levels of year-groups; and to indicate pupils who may have learning difficulties. This short list should not be read to imply that the same tests will fulfil these purposes adequately. A test which reveals a spectrum of attainments will have a different basis and structure from a test which yields data comparing the position of a pupil's score with others in a reference group. Additionally, the treatment of the data must be appropriate; for instance, when groups are considered, it is usually helpful to calculate average scores (and other statistics), so that interpretation relative to identified populations can be done. These points are dealt with in Chapter 6.

One use of transfer data which requires no action on the part of the receiving school is retention in 'the records' in case there is a need to refer to it. This kind of routine filing is really indefensible as it verges on the negligent. At the least, each set of records should be appraised by careful scrutiny and notes made on the implications of any test and other information and the decisions which ought to be considered.

Monitoring standards
The idea that it is possible to keep track of standards of pupil attainment has gained more credence in the UK over the past decade than hitherto. At its most simple, the procedure entails giving a test to an entire population and repeating the operation at intervals, so that differences between occasions can be compared. Over short timespans the method is acceptable, but when curricular or other conditions which affect the

nature of pupils' learning are changing, a test which might have been well-matched with attainments in the population on an earlier occasion may be unsatisfactory on a later occasion. (This criticism of national reading surveys surfaced in the Bullock Report, 1975.) The use of electronic calculators and computers is one example of curriculum change; less obvious are changes in vocabulary and language use (for example, 'jeans', 'prioritize', 'software'). Introducing and resourcing the teaching of the National Curriculum should produce deep-rooted changes in attainments in course of time, if only because the wide scatter of attainments of previous eras becomes narrowly focused on attainment target profiles.

In standards monitoring, however, not only must the tests accurately reflect the attainments of interest, but the population characteristics also have to be taken into account. For instance, a large influx of pupils whose mother tongue is not English might lead to a fall in average scores on a Reading test, but the sub-sample of children whose first or only language is English might well have gained a higher average score (compared with a previous occasion). When a whole population is tested, the average score (called 'the mean' by statisticians) can be computed fairly precisely. If the population is large, it would be preferable to obtain scores from a sample of pupils, which ought to be fully representative of the population and its constituent sub-populations. The result from a sample is an estimate of the actual population mean. In general, the smaller the sample, the less reliable is the estimate. It can be seen from these comments that structuring the sample(s) prior to a survey is a technical job; similarly, interpreting results which involve the comparison of estimates and inferences about the performance of populations calls for some technical know-how.

An example of how tests can be used to keep track of general standards comes from a northern LEA. This authority gave every pupil tests in Mathematics, Reading and Non-verbal Reasoning annually as Easter approached. The ages at which children were tested were nine to ten, then 11–12 and 13–14 years. Comparisons were possible between successive cohorts and between occasions at two-year intervals for each cohort. Interesting questions arose from the test averages for the first complete series, which indicated that Mathematics attainments and Non-verbal Reasoning were consistently above the national (standardization) averages, but that Reading fell from the same high level at nine to ten years to about average by age 13–14 years.

When every pupil in a population is tested or otherwise assessed, the result is a complete survey producing an exact set of parameters. The TGAT proposals are that each National Curriculum subject component will contribute to a profile; the subject panels have then proposed how components should be weighted in the assessments and, presumably, in any aggregation (for example, in Writing the weights proposed are: conveying meaning 70 per cent, spelling 20 per cent, handwriting 10 per cent). Though TGAT mainly wanted the percentages of pupils attaining each level per component to be the basis for reporting, it accepted that aggregation would be necessary to enable summaries to be made. The consequence is that with weighting included, population means and measures of dispersion will be produced; and these will probably become the focus of attention rather than the criteria and related attainments of the pupils in successive annual cohorts.

Accountability

The concepts associated with accountability have been debated at length (for example, Becher and Maclure, 1979); they range from evaluating what schools are doing through case-study and self-appraisal procedures to holding schools to account for their pupils' results on tests. In Britain this latter crude form of accountability affects secondary schools as a consequence of judgements based on external examination results. As in the case of monitoring, these judgements may be sensible when the schools are not subjected to marked changes. Thus it may be reasonable for a head teacher (or the governors) to ask for explanations of distinct variations in results compared with previous years or compared with other departments. It is less defensible for an authority to compare one school with another unless some account is taken of the differences between the schools in the circumstances which would have affected their work with the pupils throughout their school experience. Regrettably, perhaps, the TGAT proposals did not include procedures for taking differing school circumstances into account.

An extensive literature is building up on the study of school effectiveness (for example, Marks *et al.*, 1983; Gray *et al.*, 1984; Jesson, 1988). The variables which have pronounced associations with differential performance in external examinations are found to be (1) the ability levels of the pupils on arrival, (2) the proportion of lower socio-economic group pupils and (3) the proportion of higher socio-economic group pupils. When these variables are used in equations derived from studies with a large number of schools, it is possible to say (approximately) which of the schools are obtaining results in line with expectation and which fall below or above expectation. Hence schools with higher proportions of less able children at, say, seven years, but whose overall social background is lower than the average for the authority, will have this circumstance allowed for when compared with other schools whose characteristics are different. The role of tests in examining variations from estimations of predicted performance is critical because they are used to gauge the 'ability' of the pupils in relation to the criteria used to assess attainments. At the secondary level the tests most widely used have been of 11-year-olds' verbal reasoning ability, with external examinations taken as the subsequent criterion of performance.

In one authority, headteachers are being told about their standing in relation to the expectation generated by the data from all of the authority's schools. Clearly, the method outlined here goes some way towards making due allowance for school circumstances. It still leaves much that the data does not account for. One aspect of this deficiency may be that the ability measures (that is, the tests) are not the most appropriate ones.

Allocating resources
In some authorities survey testing is used as an aid to allocating additional resources to schools. The most common area is Reading (which has a larger take-up of tests than any other), though Mathematics has come on the scene in recent years with the increasing deployment of advisory teachers amongst primary schools. The technique most frequently used is to

analyse the survey results school by school as well as for the authority as a whole. The means (average scores) for each school are calculated together with the proportion of pupils falling above or below arbitrarily chosen scores at equal intervals above and below the mean respectively.

For example, if half of the population of pupils (for example, all of those in the authority's third-year primary classes) on a test with a maximum possible score of 70 obtain scores of 41 or less, and a quarter score up to 33, with three-quarters scoring up to 61, it could be decided to identify those schools with more than a quarter of their pupils scoring below 40. These schools could then be visited by an adviser/inspector to ascertain whether a good case exists for the allocation of additional, specialist teacher time. Some authorities attach a lot of importance to the test data as it provides evidence which gainsays the case put forward by forceful heads and also prompts additional action in schools where reticent heads are willing to make do without involving anyone else.

Yet another policy for which testing is integral to implementation is staffing according to curricular demands. One LEA has decided that for the first three secondary years schools should follow a model which has notional group sizes which vary according to three factors. These are: (1) subjects which can be taught to groups of 30, for example, English, Geography and Mathematics; (2) subjects which are constrained by circumstances to groups of 20, for example, workshop places and safety; and (3) the proportion of children with special educational needs, who will be taught in groups of 15. The policy is based on the recognition of an overall proportion in the LEA of 20 per cent of pupils having special needs of some kind and, furthermore, that the pupils in this category can be identified by testing and teacher quotas in each school determined accordingly.

Now that most schools are responsible for managing their own resources, test results including those from National Curriculum assessments could be used to bring attention to patterns of attainment which additional resource allocations might influence. However, schools ought to compare their own pattern with a larger sub-sample (or the population results) so as to keep variations between subjects in perspective.

Identification of pupils in specified categories

This application of test results is centred on the children as individuals. The procedure can be simple as when a single test is used or it can be highly complex when several assessments are involved. Sometimes the process is described as 'screening', usually when only one test is used to identify the pupils whose attainments or ability is much lower than the majority of the children in the population. Thus test results are used as criteria to decide whether pupils falling into specific categories should be examined further with a view to their receiving specialist teaching. Great care has to be taken whenever categories of pupil are identified because misclassification can be damaging, and in any event the 'labelling' syndrome must be avoided. Children who are labelled as members of a category are liable to receive stereotyped treatment at the expense of their individual learning needs. National testing, with its potential for the misuse of results communicated to parents in the context of the other pupils' attainments will require especially careful handling.

The most obvious categories into which children are grouped are those formally 'Statemented' and those identified in schools as experiencing significant learning difficulties, with these divided into bands according to school year or age. Other categories used are children who are in some way exceptional (for example, outstanding at Mathematics or some other accomplishment).

In some authorities a standard teaching scheme has been developed for early reading and the children's progress is measured by their attempts to show comprehension of the text by responding to pictures. According to this simple test, those children who make little or no progress are 'screened out' for more detailed assessment and specialist teaching. Any additional assessment is requested of an educational psychologist and this may lead to initiating a formal 'Statement' under the special needs procedures. The scheme described is based on the principle that additional help should be given to children who have difficulty in learning as soon as practicable. Many authorities provide screening tests for pupils in the 7+ cohort, that is, the traditional first-year Juniors. Where this is not done, schools might well consider operating formal screening procedures themselves.

Identification through the use of screening methods can only lead to the location of a proportion of children experiencing learning difficulty. There are other types of condition (such as social background and temperamental factors) which may give rise to a pupil's problems. One pupil who comes to mind did well on every scholastic test, but his temperament was unsettled to the point of hyperactivity. In his case going on test results alone would have led to neglect of his learning difficulties.

Accreditation
Up until recent years accreditation has been the almost exclusive practice of external examination bodies. There were territorial boundaries between examinations in the school and the industrial/commercial sectors, but these have started to overlap largely because the City and Guilds produced syllabuses which appealed to teachers working with pupils who were likely to obtain only a handful of low level passes in the Certificate of Secondary Education examination. Another turn of events came when the movement towards providing youngsters with a more comprehensive record of achievement during school years gained momentum in its own right and the benefit of public commendation through the pronouncements of government ministers. Then in 1983 the Oxford Delegacy for School Examinations announced that it was going to develop a system for schools to use which would provide an authenticated record of three aspects of achievement, that is, (1) external examination results, (2) other awards or marks of accomplishment and (3) personal qualities. To retain the authority of the Delegacy schools were to be recognized as 'centres', competent to handle the sections concerned with (2) and (3) above.

School-based attainment tests can find a place in this type of record, especially those which are developed in agreement with local employers. Several records of achievement projects aimed at developing guidelines with national currency started in 1985; also by then the 80 or so LEA Technical and Vocational Education Initiative projects in existence each had a 'profile' component. Taken in conjunction with the external examinations, school tests can become part of the apparatus of accreditation, depending on whether or not any extant national guidelines are satisfied. Locally devised and administered tests could be especially valuable if they employ appropriate performance tasks – in contrast with the preponderant examination board dependence upon written or multiple-choice papers.

A substantial number of LEAs now support schemes for teaching modern languages (or French only) which are designed to promote children's competence when communicating in life-like settings. These schemes follow graded objectives and pupils may take a series of graded tests. For the younger pupils the tests involve engaging in conversation with an assessor, but for older pupils reading and writing tasks are introduced. In principle, pupils can attempt any level of test whenever they are thought to be proficient enough to pass; in practice, the tests are likely to be given at a specific time, for example, as part of the school's examination work. This delay might well lessen the motivation claimed for the graded approach. The virtue is that the schools in the scheme agree on the basic curriculum, so a good match between what is taught and what is tested is made possible.

Selection
About 12 per cent of the pupils in England and Wales live in areas in which selection to grammar schools is operated by the LEA. Only a few of the 33 authorities have schemes which oblige every pupil to be considered, as parents are given the choice of opting their child into the procedure. In the larger authorities, with one exception, selection operates in isolated districts; in the small authorities with a dozen or so secondary schools all pupils are eligible for selection, usually to separate boys' and girls' grammar schools.

Essentially selection involves prediction; it is not an end in itself. The function of a selection procedure is to divide pupils into two groups. In the selected group, ideally, every member is deemed to be more suited to the type of education provided by the grammar school than every member of the rejected group. In reality, it is extremely difficult to divide a population in such a decisive way because the attributes which may be critical to success in the selective school are (1) multiple rather than singular, (2) measured on continuous scales not dichotomous categories, (3) influenced by social background, especially when obtained at interviews, and (4) subject to situational effects such as inter-school differences between teachers' ratings. Additionally, as pupils mature, other characteristics which affect scholastic performance emerge.

Selection practices typically involve the use of tests, sometimes in conjunction with teachers' ratings or interviews. These predictors can only be justified when set against acceptable criteria such as success rates at external examinations. Hence it is essential that follow-up studies are done which should include the rejected pupils as well. The reason for their inclusion is that some members of this sub-population will probably succeed at criterion levels comparable with the selected sub-population, and this information should influence judgement of the system and its modification. (For an extended discussion see Sumner, 1986.)

Target setting
There is growing interest in the idea that targets can be defined to specify what children should be able to do by a given age. And further, that setting tests focused on the targets will raise standards. In the USA, this type of test and test procedure is known as the 'minimal competency' movement, and it is practised widely, enforced by state legislation. Though the details vary, in respect of age of pupils assessed and definitions of competencies, its critics cite evidence which shows that schools and teachers concentrate their efforts on putting the largest possible number of pupils through the test(s), with the consequence that overall standards decline towards whatever has been defined as minimal. In some schemes schools and individual teachers are held accountable, so the effect described is understandable. The TGAT scheme seemingly avoids the minimal competence trap by having progressive levels. But as these have been linked with key stages defined by age, the pressure on schools (brought about by publication of results) to have all or most pupils reach the age level standard is likely to be pervasive.

To some extent, the urge to set a target can be appreciated when substantial numbers of pupils apparently leave primary or even secondary schools with only rudimentary literacy or mathematical (arithmetic) skills. In Britain, according to APU reports, this situation does not prevail and there would seem to be little point in resourcing large-scale testing programmes which effectively only assessed a small minority in respect of limited targets. A further point is that there are technical issues in 'standard setting' (what is an appropriate target?, or what is the test pass mark which certifies that a target has been reached?).

The National Curriculum working parties for Mathematics, Science and English were apparently experiencing target setting difficulties until the TGAT scheme of ten levels with subjects expressed as components offered a structure to which targets could be fitted. Even so, the targets for each 'key stage' remain very general, to the extent that setting adequate tests, to sample the domains implied (see Chapter 4) is likely to be problematic.

Internal school policies

Feedback to pupils on their learning
Tests which are based upon sections of the course are clearly the most appropriate for feedback to pupils. It follows that teachers are in the best position to decide what is closely related to the work attempted by the pupils, but there are some texts or schemes which incorporate stage or topic tests. Also there is a growing tendency for projects to be set up for the express purpose of creating carefully thought out tests which focus on skills, for example, the *Scottish Science Skills* material (Peacock, 1985). The various graded test schemes fall into this category in some respects, but in these cases the yardstick is 'the grade'.

One way in which tests are used to encourage and regulate learning is by so called 'mastery learning'. This is a process (not a teaching method or style) which requires planning to provide units of learning which define self-contained parts of the course. Each unit is followed by a test, and it is a condition of the system that each pupil must 'pass' the test in order to be allowed to study the next unit. Pupils who fail the test are given help, or are able to seek assistance with their learning using methods they choose. Those who pass the test are given enrichment assignments, mainly for their intrinsic value in extending knowledge in the field of study. The principle employed in 'mastery learning' is that knowledge of how much of a unit has been learned reasonably well gives encouragement and reinforcement, whilst the pupils who need to improve discover which aspects have to be given close attention (as does the teacher).

Protagonists of this process (for example, Black and Dockrell, 1980) claim that the pupils who have previously struggled to learn or been apathetic improve their rate of progress and depth of understanding. A cynical view is that the process has much in common with old-fashioned teaching. However, there are radical differences, in that emphasis is placed on each individual's accomplishments and specific problems; additionally, progress is regulated as well as discussed. All this is a far cry from textbook-based short tests which provided the marks for the weekly merit list, but there is a danger that adapted versions of the process might be corrupted into mark-grubbing by pupils. Allied dangers are that teachers will put most effort into securing progress at the lower-level 'core' and at the expense of providing for the more capable.

Feedback to the teacher on pupils' learning – diagnostic assessment

As well as obtaining a day-to-day ongoing appraisal of pupils' work, their progress and difficulties, teachers can get a more structured type of feedback from the analysis of test results. Teachers marking their own test papers obtain this feedback incidentally, and the details gained undoubtedly can be of value. From the standpoint of testing two developments are of interest.

One is the publication of tests designed to indicate what a pupil knows and to differentiate this from what is not known (about the domain represented by the sample of questions). Another approach is to score sections of a test to produce a set of scores each labelled according to a sub-domain. When a graphic representation of the results is used, it is often called a 'profile'. Thus for each pupil there is a profile which is interpreted as showing relative strengths and weaknesses, though certain technical problems in comparing sub-scores should be taken into account. On occasions the results for a class are added together for each sub-domain; the lower points of this group profile are taken to indicate weak areas of learning which require remedial teaching for the whole class. One set of primary mathematics tests has data in the manual on the average level of attainment of pupils in the national standardization, computed for each item in the tests; teachers can thus compare their own pupils' standards with external reference information and judge according to their own circumstances.

In many respects the profiles described above are extremely limited as diagnostic devices. The reason is that the components of the profile (that is, the sub-domains) provide descriptive information which contains no indication of the nature of pupils' learning problems. Hence any diagnosis is likely to be heavily inferential and based on a teacher's experience. In an attempt to get behind the description and relate poor attainment to learning problems new types of test have been developed. One type of test does not produce scores or sub-scores, but instead pupils' responses to each question are used as evidence to place individuals into categories. The specific categories are derived from patterns of errors and so are much more indicative of the remedial learning which should be provided. This approach has been employed on computer-administered tests which can be programmed to present sequences of questions designed to identify many patterns of erroneous response strategies and false conceptions.

An approach which is tied more closely to curriculum objectives was explored in Scotland (Black and Dockrell, 1984). A diagnostic teaching strategy was implemented through the collaboration of researchers and teachers (of French, Home Economics, Technical Studies and Geography). The strategy was similar to the mastery learning process, in that short course units were defined and tests prepared for assessing progress and indicating which pupils should have remedial teaching/learning opportunities. The types of question were defined as follows: (1) 'single act' questions which assess specific knowledge or a particular performance; (2) 'closed domain' which sample from a well-knit area of knowledge such as the ingredients and procedures used in making and baking a cake; and (3) 'open domain' involving conceptual understanding and productive rather than receptive activity. The project account shows that questions were developed for each end of unit test given as the course progressed and that the pupils had a better appreciation of the purpose for the tests as compared with traditional marking practices.

At the time of writing, rather a lot is being claimed for 'diagnostic assessment' through giving feedback based on profiles. The policy is undoubtedly soundly based in learning theory and is supported by teachers' experience. However, each of the techniques or approaches described above has a number of technical difficulties which users should look for critically. A major point is that successful diagnosis is heavily dependent on using tests which fit very closely with the curriculum *and* with children's learning characteristics.

Specific learning difficulties
As we have seen, each school should have a policy aimed at meeting the requirement to review pupils in order to detect the presence or emergence of any learning difficulties. Such a policy could well involve the pupils themselves or their parents in reporting learning problems. Implementing the policy might entail using tutorial or lesson time for self-assessment by pupils or providing time and documentation for parents to consider. Implementation could also include using a number of standardized tests and laying down rules which could enable decisions to be made about which children ought to receive further assessments. The policy should give guidance to teachers about how far preliminary appraisals of pupils might go before other professionals in the school should be brought on to the scene, and the action which the school might consider before and possibly after consulting with a pupil's parents.

A typical procedure in a primary school would be to give a year-group of children one or more standardized tests which would be used to identify pupils falling into, say, the lowest third of the score distribution obtained. These individuals would be reviewed to enable any apparent difficulties to be recorded. If the school has a specialist teacher, the first stage could lead to more intensive or specific performance assessments being made individually and specialized tests being given in appropriate cases. Should these tests show that a pupil has exceptional or persistent difficulties, the parents should be involved and consultation with specialists from outside the school initiated. It is obvious from this description of procedure that the group tests might be quite general (verbal, non-verbal, spatial and reasoning tests or Mathematics and English tests), whereas at the individual stage the tests might be concerned with quite particular attributes such as span of attention or reading sub-elements or speech, and so on. There are a number of tests which teachers with specialist training might use, and in certain instances some of the same tests would be used by educational psychologists. Many psychologists are willing to train teachers in the use of specialist appraisal techniques and tests and are keen to work collaboratively on remedying children's difficulties.

Grouping pupils
School policies on grouping are extremely varied. In primary schools, partly because published HMI reports have repeatedly drawn attention to the notion of stretching the more able pupils, it is becoming commonplace for the more advanced children to be placed into sets. One effect, of course, is to produce a lower set. The two sides of the argument are that more able children have needs that are best provided for by teaching them together as a relatively homogeneous group; or that differentiating children sets up expectations and associated methods which result in predictions which are self-fulfilling about the members of the groups.

There are certainly many difficulties inherent in the separation of children in this way, even for the so-called basic subjects of English and Mathematics. These cannot be debated here, but points for questioning would be: (1) what constitutes 'more able'? (Denton and Postlethwaite, 1985, show that high-ability identification relates to separate attainments; it is a mistake to talk globally about 'exceptional ability' for all but a very small minority of children); (2) on occasions individual teachers assess individual children idiosyncratically, should there not be agreement between teachers about children and also on what is regarded as evidence of high ability or high attainment?; and (3) with regard to seeking some confirmation which is not dependent on the teacher–pupil relationship, are suitable tests or other performances required?

In the secondary phase it seems that the differentiation of pupils early in their time at a school is becoming more accepted in place of mixed-ability grouping. The one practice which is almost universal is the placing of 'slower learners' into groups, at least for basic subjects. The remaining children can be allocated to sets, or to parallel bands which have hierarchical sets, and so on. There are some published tests of ability or attainment which can be used in banding or setting procedures. For the most part, however, the evidence for judging between pupils comes from teacher-devised tests or examinations, though these are seldom structured to allow for the inter-set or inter-band overlaps which should be examined. (Ideas about how year groups can be tested when there are different band levels of pupils are discussed in Chapter 7.)

Educational guidance

There are tests which can be used to offer pupils guidance about their choice of courses in the upper secondary stage of schooling. These tests are intended to give ancillary information to that which is available from the internal examinations, teachers' observations, National Curriculum tests, and pupils' own preferences. Tests used for guidance purposes are regarded as aptitude tests for the reason that they have been found to correlate with subsequent performance in different subjects or training courses. On this account the user can base the advice given to the pupil on the levels of success achieved by pupils in similar samples who obtained higher or lower scores (as described in Chapter 6). The kinds of test which schools might use as indicators of aptitude are usually tests of different sorts of ability. These involve the comprehension of verbal or diagrammatic material related to tasks involving components of deductive or inductive reasoning. The range of tests available is shown by their titles: verbal, numerical, spatial, mechanical, clerical, scientific, critical thinking, abstract thinking, perceptual, motor and dexterity.

It should be borne in mind also that educational guidance can arise from the interpretation of results from tests administered to pupils at many ages and for many purposes. In this sense the results are used to raise questions about how to approach a child's education. For example, a counselling inventory, personality questionnaire or attitude scale might be administered by teachers who have received appropriate training and then interpretation of results brought into a discussion with the pupil and parent together.

Schools which have developed careers education resources may adopt the policy of linking career interests with educational guidance. In this case careers inventories can be used which will indicate the occupational areas and levels which a pupil could consider as one of several possibilities. For instance, a pupil with interests in medical care would be advised about the educational options which would suit studying to qualify as a doctor, as a nurse, a pathologist, and so on. Computer-based systems are coming into widespread use with pupils' questionnaire responses providing the raw material (Closs, 1980).

Curriculum improvement

Very few schools would deny having a policy aimed at improving the curriculum – possibly as a whole but more probably in parts. In fact governing bodies have certain responsibilities with regard to the curriculum and many LEAs have prepared school review guidelines which include questions about the appropriateness of the curriculum and the assessment of pupils' learning. As shown earlier by reference to the Scottish diagnostic teaching project, there is a growing realization that assessment should not merely constitute an additional component. Rather assessment should be integral to the course, so the first requirement is that it should reflect its aims and *the activities* it embodies.

For example, in one locality a project with several schools involved has developed problem-solving strategies in Mathematics. The course activity is planned for small groups of children working collaboratively at devising problems as well as solving them. Clearly, assessment of some kind is necessary to show whether this approach promotes problem solving strategies and concepts among some or all of the pupils. It follows also that adapting the trial curriculum in the light of the feedback from pupils will depend more on hunches than informed judgement unless valid indications of pupils' contributions are obtained. At the time of writing, the teachers appear satisfied that their informed observations and conversations with pupils will provide enough information for adapting the course. But some have inquired whether or not there are published tests available which would be reliable and valid. The answer is that there do not appear to be any, and that there may be scope for developing materials for publication if the experience of the sample of pupils involved in the project can be generalized to specified populations, especially in respect of activities and questions.

The outcomes of curriculum improvement efforts should be assessed from two perspectives. One is feedback on the nature of the pupils' learning, given the new materials and teaching methods (for example, what does a class learn from a technology project on propulsion?). The other is concerned with more general attainments, motivation and skills. For example, compared with control groups, pupils who had followed a new humanities curriculum were found to be more highly motivated towards schoolwork and to have higher reading test scores.

Who wants testing?

This question is guaranteed to raise a smile at teachers' meetings on assessment. When it is posed as a serious question, brows begin to wrinkle. One teacher who did not attempt to answer said, 'The nearer you get to testing, the less you want to have anything to do with it'. There is something in this notion, in that parents are often keen to have their children tested, whereas the children may not be so enthusiastic. And only a few years ago a government minister for education was publicly advocating that tests of minimal standards should be compulsory for all children; and the TGAT structure of tests and assessments has been the outcome.

However, in my own experience a substantial proportion of children have said that tests were interesting and enjoyable to do. When the results are promised beforehand, the motivation of pupils can be very high, especially when the purpose is explained fully and the conditions under which the tests are done are understood. Even pupils who are usually uncooperative have been fully involved when the object of testing was their own educational guidance. Parents also tend to support testing when their offspring's future is up for consideration. In these instances there is no clash of interest: the clients are the pupils and the testers are acting professionally in their best interests. The same case applies to testing which is carried out for diagnostic purposes. In fact teachers express more interest in diagnostic testing than that for any other purpose because it supports their efforts to promote learning.

An example of confusion about testing purpose comes from an authority's efforts to set up a procedure for assessing pupils to assist with their transition from one phase of schooling to another. The panel convened to devise a procedure proposed that the children should complete a set of modular tests from mid-May to mid-June with results being sent to the secondary schools by July. The primary school heads had accepted that the purpose was to give to the secondary teachers an up-to-date picture of each pupil's attainments. However, after several meetings during the modular test development phase the primary heads made a case for administering the modules before Easter on the ground that 'their' teachers would want to have time for remedial work with the less capable children.

As we have seen, the reasons for testing ought to relate to educational ends. Confusion or misunderstandings arise from several sources, principally lack of definition of policies and lack of communication of policies which exist. Confusion occurs most probably because too much is required of a testing programme.

One LEA which instituted a testing programme extending from seven-year-old primary pupils to 14-year-old secondary pupils wished the results to be used by (1) the schools to examine children's progress and identify those who might have learning difficulties, (2) the education committee who seemingly wished to be able to compare individual schools annually and with other schools for any one year, (3) the teachers to obtain diagnostic information about individual pupils, (4) the parents as a basis for discussing with teachers their child's progress or lack of it, (5) the advisers and psychologists to allocate specialist support teachers and (6) the officers to monitor the service. Some of the tests were of attainment in reading and mathematics, others were of abilities in verbal and non-verbal reasoning. The secondary third year pupils were given a set of tests designed to assist with the choice of option courses in the fourth year. The teachers through their unions and representatives on the education committee raised objections to the 'blanket' testing of pupils according to this programme. They focused their criticism on the proposal to supply committee members with the detailed school-by-school analyses, saying they would be used to make criticisms of schools without allowances made for the social background of each, or of particular educational circumstances, for example, school closures and re-organization, subjects taught without specialist teachers, incidence of pupils with learning difficulties, and so on.

Apart from the statistical aspects of making proper interpretations of differences found between schools, it was clear that the nature of each of the tests and the limitations these imposed on their use, had not been appreciated. Nor had there been any attempt to formulate educational policies clearly, so that the separate purposes relevant to each year group could be appreciated. For example, at 7+ a reading test was to be used for 'screening' – but what does this policy really mean? At 8+ a Mathematics test was given for 'diagnosis' – again it was assumed that teachers understood the policy. Furthermore, it became clear that diagnosis meant that successful remediation would inevitably follow, in the minds of some of those supporting testing, despite the fact that the 'medical model' does not always lead to this outcome.

Why these situations occur is readily appreciated by considering the secondary-level guidance tests. The policy here is that schools will be enabled to supplement their existing knowledge of each pupil with a number of test results which can be used to assist in decision-making about fourth-year optional subjects. This policy was implemented by the authority purchasing and supplying the materials and training a test administrator from amongst the teachers of each school. The task, then, was to administer the tests and interpret the results in conjunction with the results from school examinations, information from records and pupils' statements as to preferences amongst the options available. However, schools were required to send the results on prepared forms to the education office, so that a standardization for the authority's population could be computed. But the mixture of motives in play was very evident because a school-by-school analysis was to be prepared for all tests in the authority's programme (primary and secondary) for presentation to the education committee. Clearly, this latter analysis has nothing to do with the implementation of the policy to give educational guidance to individual pupils.

The illustration given above shows that policies can become diffuse or entangled despite the good intentions of the people responsible. A practical difficulty with making use of test results in several ways is that the more closely a test is suited to one purpose, the less satisfactory it is likely to be for any other. For example, a single reading test which produces an indicator of a child's reading standard is unsuitable for a survey intended to show what levels of competency are found across a range of reading tasks appropriate to children of a certain age.

Authorities usually make decisions about tests and testing through consultation carried out with a panel composed of teachers, psychologists and officers. These groups often seek advice on test suitability from publishers or independent bodies. For the most part, the methods whereby these panels work are exemplary; publishers are contacted to obtain specimen sets of tests and current prices, so that whatever materials are available can be compared. Occasionally trial runs are organized to 'see how the test goes down' (rather like medicine) and data are obtained from the analysis of pupils' scripts. However, at the vital point of choosing between one test and another panel members concentrate on test content and layout instead of giving detailed scrutiny to the information supplied in test manuals or results derived from test analyses.

In good manuals the range of purposes which a test could fulfil should be specified, but whatever the test author might claim, the onus for correct use rests with the user. Furthermore, the manual should make clear whether or not training in testing is desirable or whether training with the particular test is required. But these are secondary considerations; the user's most important task is to clarify the policy which justifies making assessments and to ensure that the main purpose is not prejudiced by secondary purposes claiming a higher priority. They can then go on to plan how to obtain the information they require in the most effective way (as proposed in a structured way in Chapter 9). In doing so they should consider a range of assessment materials from the standpoints of what they assess, how accurately they measure and in what ways the results can be applied.

CHAPTER 3
The Scope of Tests

In this chapter the term 'test' is taken to include inventories, structured tasks for observation, questionnaires and rating scales because these types of instrument have features in common with formally constructed tests, as described later in Chapter 7; also a more rounded view of pupils and their learning circumstances is made accessible by accepting this more inclusive notion of a test. The scope of tests is considered from two standpoints, that is, concepts related to measurement, and classification of tests according to the type of behaviour assessed.

Tests as measures of attributes

Measurement takes place when a 'quality' is quantified. Even a 'more' or 'less' distinction counts because the pupils are ordered into two sets. Grading systems, whether based on teachers' observations or judgements of a performance or upon test and examination marks, are all forms of the same type of measure, i.e. *ordinal scaling*. It is most obvious when pupils are given a rank order: 1st, 2nd, 3rd, . . ., nth. Other examples are letters: A, B, C, etc.; accept/reject; and upper, middle, lower. Thus ordinal scales show relative position only.

Ordinal scales are less sophisticated than *interval scales*, in which a score is awarded by totalling points representing increments of the quality assessed. The equal intervals, usually of 1 point, which these scales utilize can be misleading, at least to the unwary. For instance, if in an English examination one pupil was awarded 40 marks and another 80 marks, it is not possible to say that the former was only half as good at English as the latter; only that his/her *score* was a half. Neither could it be said that a pupil with 60 marks is as far below the one with 80 marks as he/she is above the pupils with 40 marks; only that there was a 20-mark difference either way.

Measurement with an interval scale is the most common type in education. It is often treated as if it is *ratio scaling.* As the name implies, one score twice the magnitude of another means two times the quality assessed (for example, 2000 mm jumped is twice 1000 mm).

Ratio scales are devised and used for educational measurement, but their interpretation is not as straightforward as it is for physical dimensions, as instanced above. Test scores represent *to some extent* the attributes developed by individuals. Whilst a great deal is made of the idea that only a single dimension is embodied in a scale, it is exceedingly difficult to demonstrate that there are no qualitative differences in an attribute at various score points. For example, whilst the measurement of height is generally agreed to be uni-dimensional, the attributes required to jump over a barrier half a metre high are very different from those needed to clear 2 metres. Furthermore, making a gain of 20 mm at the lower height is vastly different from the same measured achievement at the higher level.

The point about qualitative changes underlying changes in measured attributes applies to each of the three types of scale. It is, however, of crucial importance that it should be kept in view because of the tendency to shift attention from attribute assessment to scores and their statistical manipulation. In fact, a test is a situation which elicits some kind of performance from each person who takes it; though the sample of tasks presented to each person may be the same, there is no way of knowing whether each respondent performs the tasks set by the test in the same manner. In other words it is not possible to measure an attribute directly. Therefore, test scores are best thought of as reflections or images of attributes. And because test questions are samples from hypothesized populations of questions the image obtained will be more or less accurate and, in a good test, sufficient to rely on (cf. photographic images and readings given by the instruments in a car).

The definition of types of measurement is critical to an appreciation of what test results show. Tests or standardized assessment tasks are designed to elicit responses to questions; these responses may be used to classify pupils either into categories or into levels. Examples of categories are: extrovert/introvert; serialist/holist; concrete operation/abstract operation; special needs/ordinary needs; convergent thinking/divergent thinking; motivated by status/rewards/peer influence/intellectual stimulation/pleasure. It can be seen that some of these distinctions imply a 'more or less' differentiation, so that a person can be placed on a continuum, for instance, as midway between 'highly extrovert' and 'highly introvert'. There is no implication that being at one point on the continuum is good in some way unless there is firm evidence that, say, introverts always do better at examinations and extroverts do better as public entertainers.

When measurements imply 'level', there is an implication that higher is better. Thus when scores on a test are summed, the aggregation is supposed to relate to qualitative changes in the attribute assessed. In much of the literature on assessment the idea is stressed that a measure should be uni-dimensional, that is, should refer to a single 'pure' trait. Such a concept seems to be an over-simplification; it would imply that a given increment of score corresponds to a precise amount of an attribute rather like adding n sugar cubes to a pile means the increase of n units of sugar. A better analogy, as illustrated above, would be the measurement of height in jumping; the dimension used may be feet or millimetres, but an increment of n units has a different meaning (when applied to the attribute of jumping attainment in a population of people) according to its position in the scale relative to the zero point of ground level.

The score or category awarded to a child shows performance on the day. For some children the sample of questions in a test might be a good match with capability on the day, as predicted by experience, learning and preparedness, so the result in these cases would be the optimum one. For most test takers the result is likely to be somewhat lower than optimal, but there is no way of knowing to what extent any individual's result differs from their 'true' optimum. For this reason it is preferable to regard a test result as an estimate of performance and to report it as such (see Chapter 5).

Of course, test users have to consider fully whether a particular test sample of items (questions *and* responses) matches the domain they wish to assess. Test constructors can help a great deal in this respect by laying out the specification used to define the domain that the test is intended to assess. In some tests the specification may be simple (for example, for a clerical ability test of placing numbers in rank order, ten items could deal with lists containing integers between 0 and 10, ten with integers between 0 and 50, ten items would be in the form x.y and ten of the form x.yz when x, y and z can have values between 1 and 9). In general, test specifications are not defined clearly for the users by test authors. On occasions quite complex schemes for sampling item populations can be built into the test domain using cross-classifications (for example, skills of addition, subtraction, multiplication and division cross-classified by whole numbers, decimals and letters for numbers; four skills for each of three numerical modes gives 12 sub-populations of items). The score obtained by a pupil depends very greatly on many other factors. But in so far as the specification says how a domain was sampled in order to evoke responses arising from a hypothesized attribute, it is possible to interpret sensibly the measurement(s) accruing from the test situation.

The foregoing has indicated that the measurement of human attributes is very different from the measurement of physical dimensions. There are some parallels, in that physical performance is enhanced by training and experience and also by mental effort. In a similar manner pupils will be enabled to enhance their attributes through learning experiences and their related test performance by the rehearsal of test situations. The whole object of educational assessment is distorted, however, by coaching pupils at tests rather than promoting learning which enhances skills and understandings. Furthermore, the test preparation atmosphere and conditions at the time of testing can affect pupils' performance adversely, so that the measure obtained is less than optimal. So it is preferable to think of a pupil as interacting with a test rather than merely responding to questions or tasks. For example, it can be shown that some pupils tend to perform better than others at multiple-choice question papers. A measurement from a test, therefore, contains various components some of which reflect the attribute more or less accurately and others of which arise from the test situation or materials (that is, interference or 'noise'), together with some which are the product of misconceptions or inappropriate efforts to respond (that is, errors).

Classification of tests by attributes

The term attribute has been used as an apposite general concept. It has a positive ring about it which is fitting to education and its thrust towards developing individual achievements: 'what is achievement?' In the context of learning it is appropriate to think of what a pupil has understood and can do, what the pupil has *attained*.

It is well known that attainment is influenced by factors related to circumstance and factors centred in the individual child. Though usually attention has focused primarily on 'ability', nowadays it is recognized that motivation, attitudes and study methods have a significant role in mediating attainment. Achievement, then, can be viewed as change in level and quality of attainment mediated by circumstantial variables and individual variables related to abilities, motivation, attitudes and study methods. The major variables are indicated in Figure 3.1. The diagram illustrates that personal, school and social circumstances, on the one hand, and factors related to the individual person, his/her values and response to home influences all bear upon school achievement. A detailed listing of variables in the categories amenable to assessment by testing is not practicable, but some idea of the scope embraced by each category is shown by the selection given below.

Abilities

In the context of intelligence and its assessment abilities relevant to education have been studied since early in this century. At one stage, different aspects of intelligence were tested and the results used to give a single intelligence quotient. Though controversial for many years, it is now accepted that different kinds of ability should be assessed and their education implications interpreted more specifically than was possible with a single IQ figure, (see, for example, Denton and Postlethwaite, 1985, for evidence on the identification of children deemed to be gifted in some way). Another change has accompanied the decline in acceptability of a single measure of intelligence (the IQ), in that it is no longer believed that intelligence is an innate, fixed capacity (Stott, 1983). However, it is undoubtedly the case that different measures of intelligence tend to be positively related within a population. The degree of association found leads to the notion that a general factor from a common strand is complemented by a range of specialized, distinct abilities. From the standpoint of an individual, assessing the distinctive aspects of intelligence is likely to provide information about previous development and future prospects. The recent tests published for use by educational psychologists have a broad range of scales (there are 23 tests in the *British Ability Scales*, see Elliott, Murray and Pearson, 1983) which can be used flexibly to examine a span of abilities or to look intensively at one or two.

The group tests of abilities, which are appropriate for use in schools, contain a smaller range of scales, though over several tests their spread is quite considerable. Many of the published materials available to schools consist of batteries made up of several tests scaled in the same way. The principal types of ability tests are described below.

Verbal

In these tests a measure of reasoning using verbal modes of thought and knowledge of language is obtained using questions which do not depend on specific curricula (textbooks, topics, discussion, and so on). Common question types are antonyms, synonyms, letter codes, sequences (for example, puddle, pond,

Figure 3.1:   Classification of achievement-related variables

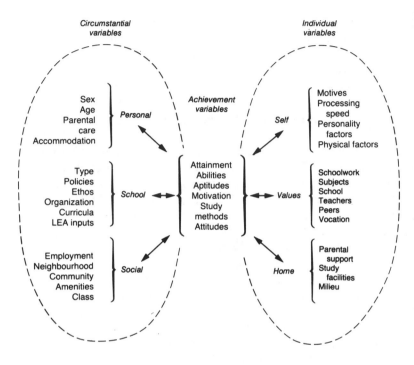

lake, ?), similes, word puzzles (for example, anagram of 'RATS', or adding a letter to complete one word which starts another word, for example, 'BUN(?)AP'), alphabetical order, deduction from propositions and deduction from data.

Non-verbal or symbolic
Typically tests of non-verbal ability present reasoning tasks through the medium of diagrams. Some of the tasks presented are the same as in verbal tests: that is, series or sequences (of shapes or orientation); similarities (for example, open or closed line diagrams); opposites (for example, symbol combination vs decomposition); deduction from diagrammatic data; and completion and combination of diagrams. Other kinds of tasks are peculiar to the use of diagrams: that is, deduction of two-dimensional matrix completions and interpreting topological diagrams. Items in tests of this kind should not require fine

visual discrimination or pose tasks which are spatial in their demands. However, it is quite common to find both types in the same test, as illustrated in Figure 3.2.

Figure 3.2: **Examples of symbolic reasoning items**

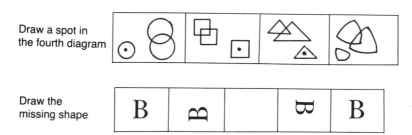

One test which has both types of item in it is called an 'abstract reasoning' test, but this label is somewhat misleading as practically all visually presented tests embody abstractions (that is, printed words and numbers, diagrams).

Perceptual
Usually, these tests are intended for use with younger children or older ones with learning difficulties. Again the items are diagrammatic, and the tasks involve inspection of a drawing and the identification of a feature or, alternatively, identification of an oddity or mismatch with a model. Examples are shown in Figure 3.3.

Figure 3.3: **Examples of perceptual test items**

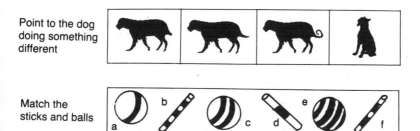

Numerical or quantitative
In the tests of numerical ability item types are divided mainly between questions about number concepts and questions based on computation. Thus tasks include: completion of number series; identification of smallest and largest numbers in a set; analogies (for example, as 10 is to 20, so is — to 60); ordinal and cardinal numbers; equalities (for example, 7 + 20 = 19 + ?); estimation; computation in various formats and combinations of operations; and 'word problems' including translation to numbers and operations (usually with simple arithmetic computations). When tests are labelled 'quantitative', item content emphasizes measures in common use such as length, area, money, time and weight.

Spatial
Tests of spatial ability are intended to assess a person's performance at tasks which involve: the visualization of objects from given points of view; movement and re-orientation of the viewpoint; rotation of the object viewed; shift of object; decomposition of figures into shapes; combination of figures into composites; discernment of shapes against background (for example, embedded figures); mirror images and reflection of shapes; projections from shapes and solids (for example, shadows cast by sunlight); enlargements and reductions; and visual acuity (that is, judgement of shape by eye). Tests can be biased towards reasoning in spatial modes, by using items which embody serialization or sequencing, similar shapes and opposites, and syllogisms. Alternatively, tests can stress mental imagery by presenting views of objects related to tasks such as identifying cross sections or aerial views, and so on. Most spatial tests are printed, and so for three-dimensional representation involve reduction to two-dimensional drawings. In individual tests objects such as cubes with diagrams on the sides can be given to the children to handle and view or to arrange.

Mechanical
Two main approaches to assessing mechanical abilities are (1) to present physical tasks which require the assembly of articles from a selection of parts (when the manipulative component is undemanding) and (2) to examine mechanical principles

(levers, pulleys, beams, friction, structures, fluid pressures, flotation, gravity). In printed tests the form of presentation is usually diagrammatic. Some tests present principle-type questions in the context of machines, so use drawings showing cranks, cogs, pipes and pistons and similar components; other tests depict real-life situations (for example, aeroplane dropping object) to present applied physics at elementary levels.

Clerical

The two aspects of clerical ability most commonly assessed are (1) speed and (2) accuracy. In speed test tasks which are conceptually simple are presented within tight time limits (for example, cross out number 2 and number 6 in all of the lines of numbers on the page; 1 0 7 3 2 5 8 7 5 6, etc.). In contrast, accuracy tests have generous time limits. Items involve the following: checking for discrepancies in lists; assigning codes according to rules; changing codes from one system to another; listing in alphabetical order; matching code shapes to letters (cf. shorthand). This last example illustrates the analogy with office skills built into many clerical ability tests.

Scientific

The intention in tests of this kind is to assess reasoning using scientific processes to infer principles. Items are written to supply the pupil taking the test with the information and premises necessary, so that the influence of learning specific curricula is minimized. Presentation utilizes diagrams of situations or phenomena, tabulated data and flow charts. Some questions may be designed to examine whether a pupil can appreciate what data is necessary to support a conclusion and so sort out superfluous information from the essential. Tests of science processes in laboratory situations have been developed by the APU science monitoring teams (Driver *et al.*, 1982). These call for observation, experimentation by changing variables, hypothesizing and deduction from data. As yet, tests of this kind have not been presented as ability measures. Another approach (Shayer *et al.*, 1979) to assessing abilities related to learning science is to test conceptual development in line with the scheme originated by Piaget, which has stages from 'intuitive thought' through 'concrete operations' to 'formal operations'. Items involve the use of materials and science apparatus, and the result is that pupils are classified according to the stages or their degree of transition from one to another.

Language
As distinct from verbal ability, though not separate or unrelated, language learning may be considered to tap abilities in which discrimination in the aural and oral fields are important. Test items may use familiar sounds, such as spoken numbers, in unusual ways (for example, to assess aural learning) or unfamiliar material (for example, symbolic script and 'made-up' spoken words to assess audio-visual association). Presentation usually is by tape recorded speech and occasionally responses may be tape recorded, though multiple-choice printed answer sheets are generally favoured.

Dexterity
Tests in this category are aimed at assessing manipulative skills developed in the upper limbs. Items involve apparatus which is grouped, placed, pushed, rotated, etc., with a single hand or using both hands in coordination. Some tests show lateral dominance or preference, and this is important for assessing cross-laterality.

Comments on ability testing

The outlines of ability tests given above show that some of the types of ability are related to particular kinds of activity, and so have an affinity with attainments. Earlier in this century a great deal of effort went into identifying 'pure' factors associated with intelligent activity. By the 1940s Vernon's (1971) distinction between the verbal – educational and practical abilities had gained widespread acceptance and the notion that reasoning capacities were fixed for any one person and determined by heredity had not been seriously challenged.

Contemporary views of abilities are that some underlying physiological attributes influence the learning which differentiates one person from another. These attributes concern neurological efficiency, memory storage and retrieval and the functions associated with brain hemispheres. Whilst the physiology is determined by inheritance, the attributes related to them are none the less modifiable. Their influence is evidenced in tasks concerned with speed of handling information and strategies for its effective processing.

Whereas speed seems more obvious and measurable, there are innumerable questions about processing. Some explanations are being put forward, for example, analogical reasoning can be characterized (Sternberg, 1985) in terms of components. These are *encoding* perceived information (by retrieving from long-term memory); *inferring* relationship in the leading proposition (for example, Lawyer is to client); *mapping* to the second, incomplete proposition; *applying* the relationship to the consequent proposition (for example, Doctor is to ?); *comparing* any options (for example, patient, casualty, accident, medicine); *justifying* the selected response; and *responding* appropriately (that is, communicating an encoded message). Similar chains of activity apply to other reasoning tasks such as linear syllogisms (that is: If A:B and B:C then C:?), seriation, set inclusion and making comparisons.

What is interesting is that, from the perspective of components, the different ability test categories as described here delineate *mode* of cognitive functioning. It hardly needs arguing that learning in a mode is integral to cognition; that is, any verbal learning enhances verbal ability to some extent. For example, extending vocabulary range and conceptual understanding (for example, what does a lawyer do, and for whom?; what does a doctor do, and for whom?) involves certain of the components. The analogy between lawyer and doctor draws on the concepts in a highly specific and limited way to pinpoint the *inferred relationship* which is common to both. In fact this component, the relational one, appears to be at the nub of concept attainment (Bruner, Goodnow and Austin, 1956).

It can be appreciated that the distinction between ability and attainment assessment is one of context, especially when there is reference to reasoning and intelligence. In ability tests, then, emphasis is placed on various components (encoding, inferring, mapping, applying, comparing, justifying and responding) in certain modes when curriculum contexts are weak. In contrast, attainment tests are predominantly about *learned relationships* in curriculum fields. Hence when curriculum-based learning is generalized cognitively, abilities are enhanced accordingly.

The foregoing commentary shows that an ability assessment should be regarded as an indicator of the reasoning capability developed by the pupil up to the time of the assessment. In so far as ability measures can be shown to relate to subsequent measures of attainments, ability tests can be regarded as indicators of aptitudes, as discussed below. Ability measures should not be accepted as indicators of capacity to learn a curriculum, for it is clear that further learning experiences – especially relational ones – could alter both ability and attainment. The commentary also shows why ability and attainment tests which share the same mode, such as written language, tend to correlate highly. In addition it shows why the interpretation of discrepancy between ability and attainment test scores can be extremely problematic.

Aptitudes

Tests in the 'Aptitude' category assess abilities or attainments or other attributes which are supposed to show predisposition to achieve in a new field. For example, a test of pitch discrimination based on listening to sounds created by electronic devices could be an aptitude test for pupils learning to play a musical instrument for which the pitch is controlled by the player, for example, a violin. Alternatively, good performance at such a test might indicate aptitude for speaking a foreign language with good intonation. The question: 'aptitude for what?', should be answered by studies which relate the abilities assessed to performance later on in the particular field of study concerned.

The abilities which have been described can be used as indicators of aptitude provided there are good grounds for doing so. Evidence to this effect should be gained from use; theory is not sufficient. For example, if spatial ability is to be used to give pupils guidance as to their aptitude for technical studies with a high content of practical work including drawing and the interpretation of diagrams, several studies which demonstrate association between spatial test results and the technical examination would be desirable. The design of these studies too should include other predictor variables such as non-verbal reasoning, previous attainment in school technical studies, mathematics, science and possibly verbal reasoning. For the spatial test to have credibility and utility the relationship with the technical examinations (obtained after a period of study) that form the criterion should be quite high. It should also be better than the relationship found with the other measures of ability; this result would support the claim that spatial ability was particularly apt as a predictor for the course.

Some of the best predictors of aptitude for a course of study are previous attainments or attainment tests given to candidates wishing to be considered for an opportunity. Various examples come to mind such as: Woodwork and Metalwork at CSE and O-level relating to courses in Further Education in vehicle mechanics, engineering and electrical installation; graded music examinations (which can be taken at any age) relating to entry into music college, special coaching schemes and county youth orchestras; English and Mathematics tested at the end of the primary stage correlating more highly than other measures with the same subjects in comprehensive schools tested two years afterwards.

When the new course of study has few obvious connections with earlier studies, prior attainment may not be particularly helpful. A striking example, with older students, was the prediction of success in practical dentistry from a test of carving a piece of chalk to resemble a given shape. Another illustration (from industry) was a test consisting of connecting coloured wires with screws given with a drawing showing the layout positioned in the open lid of the test box. This test was given to unskilled applicants for wiring assembly work.

In schools the guidance and decisions are not as specific as in the examples cited. There are some aptitude test batteries which teachers might wish to use, mainly with secondary-age pupils (publishers' catalogues give details). However, teachers should conduct trials to satisfy themselves that the aptitude indicators are valid in respect of the courses they teach. An unusual example of doing so came to notice in Wales, where a test of aptitude for learning a modern language (Carroll and

Sapon, 1955–9) was used to identify pupils whose first language was English and who could take on the additional task of learning Welsh.

Aptitude testing can be useful in advising pupils and parents about educational prospects and decisions. However, it is imperative to bear in mind that tests cannot predict with absolute certainty. When tests are used as selection devices, they are functioning as predictors of attainment and the questions as to whether the predictions are borne out are generally complex. Some approaches to following up aptitude assessments are dealt with in Chapter 6.

Motivation

There are probably no tests of motivation in use in schools at the present time in the UK despite the widespread acknowledgement that motivating pupils is the concern of schools; and also is a major reason given by the DES (1984) for promoting the development of Records of Achievement. The major aspects recognized are: (1) intrinsic and extrinsic motivation; (2) the influence of individual personality factors; and (3) tendencies to study in certain ways, for example, syllabus bound vs syllabus free (being tied to the course of study compared with setting the course in a wider field of inquiry) and serialist vs holist (studying bit by bit compared with scanning the field of study then filling in the parts). These tendencies can be attributed in part to individual make-up, and in part to previous experience of didactic as compared to heuristic methods of teaching.

One approach which I have devised to examining motives relating to school was based on extensive interviews with a sample of pupils and the analysis of essays about making effort in school written by another large sample (Sumner, 1976). The factors identified as important were described as follows: *reward* (response to tokens and praise/sanctions); *intellectual* (urge to extend understanding via relationships conveyed through abstractions represented by symbols); *enjoyment* (schoolwork that is appealing and amusing, in content and activity); *sociability* (work done in collaboration with others or in company with others); *status* (opportunities to gain approval from peers or relevant adults); *self-realization* (development and enhancement of self-concept – when this is well established, it becomes self-actualization, that is, working towards one's own goals). It can be seen that some of these factors lean towards features external to the pupil (extrinsic), whilst others gain their impetus from factors located within the pupil (intrinsic). However, all of the factors were seen as highly relevant to the population of secondary school pupils and no greater value was attached to intrinsic than extrinsic components. A questionnaire designed to assess individual differences amongst pupils for these factors has been used to evaluate *groups* for their motivational characteristics at the outset of schemes to enhance pastoral and tutorial provision in school and at later points as the scheme progressed.

The literature on personality and scholastic achievement is extensive, yet there are no tests or techniques sufficiently well developed to be brought into widespread use. Undoubtedly the authors of some personality questionnaires would disagree, but they would also press the case for anyone using their test to study a particular theory of personality and also to qualify specifically to use their materials. Perhaps the best-established personality factors are (a) extroversion vs introversion and (b) stability vs emotionality, with (c) conscientiousness vs casualness close behind. Research established several tendencies, for example, higher academic attainment at secondary level was associated with introversion, emotionality and conscientiousness, though the pattern for primary-age children was not the same (Rushton, 1976). In contrast, achievement in practical/technical subjects was more related to stability and extroversion. However, the levels of correlation found are not sufficient for firm inferences to be drawn and used in counselling youngsters, except when extreme scores are obtained (and this by only a small fraction of pupils).

The type of test alluded to here has been described because (i) computerized administration and methods for scoring complex sets of personality variables are being developed. These *apparently* make the knowledge to be gained about individual pupils far more accessible; and (ii) pressures of many kinds (for example, a wish to understand and help individuals develop; extension of specialist counselling) will probably lead teachers in the direction of personality assessment. Should this occur, it will behove anyone concerned to demand *clear* evidence that pupils have benefited from a particular assessment.

A measure of achievement motivation which has attracted a great deal of interest is called *Need for Achievement*, or *N'ach* (McClelland, 1961; Heckhausen, 1967). Whether or not a person is influenced by the motive is measured by their responses to 'thematic apperception' test drawings; these depict situations such as a boy looking at a violin. If the person being assessed describes the situation as giving rise to 'hope of success' as contrasted with 'fear of failure', scores for *N'ach* would be high. This measure might be helpful in counselling older pupils, but like the other motivational variables, it is not suited to widespread use or to group assessment. The same remarks apply to measures related to syllabus free vs syllabus bound or serialist vs holist variables.

Attitudes

These are belief systems built up by individuals about situations, objects or institutions, so of course can include all of those in the constellation of people and systems that constitute the educational milieu. Attitudes can be assessed with a variety of questionnaire types, which employ different techniques for eliciting pupils' views. Some questionnaires employ items which are quite straightforward to understand and respond to. One widely used format has questions couched as a statement accompanied by a scale arranged from 'Strongly agree' to 'Strongly disagree' (variants are 'Very true for me' to 'Not true for me', 'Always' to 'Never', etc.). Attitude scales can then be compiled from a sample of statements relevant to a topic, for example:

Pupils in this school work very hard	SA	A	D	SD
Few people here bother with homework	SD	D	A	SA
In library periods we just chat	SD	D	A	SA
When we talk in class, it's about work	SA	A	D	SD

These items have been given to illustrate how a Likert scale can tap attitudes towards schoolwork. Before being used for a serious purpose, such as evaluating attitudes in schools engaged on curriculum development schemes, a large number of questions would be tried out and analytical methods used to refine the scale. The scale score is the sum of the numerical values assigned to the SA to SD responses (note that there is a mixture of positive statements *and* negative statements linked to SA or SD responses; this is done to prompt thought and discourage routine answer ticking).

Attitude scales have been very widely used in research and are now becoming more accepted in schools for the assessment of *groups* of pupils. The list of topics is extensive; it includes: Mathematics (difficulty, usefulness, enjoyment; Foxman *et al.*, 1985); Science (interest, science in society, science teachers, science activities, Skurnik *et al.*, 1971); Technology (career in industry, technology and society, training, school technology; Page and Nash, 1980; Roat *et al.*, 1987); themes such as people who influence schooling (teachers, friends, parents); school ethos (lessons, pastoral work, aims); school organization (timetable, societies, discipline, homework); vocational interests; preferences for areas of study (language, aesthetics, outdoor/PE, mathematics, science, practical/technical, humanities); and scales such as 'importance of doing well', ' "other" image in class', 'academic self-image' and 'attitude to class' (Barker-Lunn, 1970). When analysis shows that the responses from various topic scales can be aggregated without incorporating contradictory factors, overall measures of attitude towards school can be formed.

There is a variety of formats for obtaining information about attitudes and interests, one of which is the 'open-ended question' inviting pupils to write what they think or feel. There are, however, matters of propriety and ethics to be taken into account. Consider which would be more acceptable:

(a) Interesting teachers are ones who [Answer by ticking one or more statements if you think they are true]

    (i)   encourage us to ask questions;
    (ii) use videos to get us talking;
    (iii) explain clearly and give notes;
    (iv) stick to the course.

Or (b) The most interesting teacher is one who _____

[Complete the sentence in your own words]

Instruments such as these could have a place in pupils' self-assessments as part of a counselling programme. As such, they would deserve careful preparation and sensitive interpretation to avoid detrimental results. In particular, the tentative nature of the information would have to be stressed. In this respect it is no more different than other expressions of belief or feeling; but the use of a prepared device to sample and assess might imply that the result is definitive. Assessment through conversations or informal interviews might be preferable in view of these reservations.

Study methods

Questionnaires or inventories which appraise study skills and habits have been published for many years and have been used in research. Nowadays, when the curriculum includes 'learning how to learn', it is important that pupils review their procedures and find ones which are effective. The results from instruments designed to survey study methods could be used for counselling and personal development rather than allocating pupils to high- or low-score groups. Topics dealt with can include place of study, use of time, organization, reading skills, note-taking, examination techniques, collaborative work and taking part in discussion. Another approach to study methods is to assess so-called study skills. The areas tested include use of maps and diagrams, interpretation of tables and graphs, use of reference materials (dictionary, almanacs); manipulative, recording and measurement skills; and critical thinking.

Attainments

In the UK attainment tests deal mainly with the basic areas of Reading and English, Mathematics and Number, though there are also tests in French and Science (McCall and Bryce, 1982). Up to a decade ago the tests were predominantly 'norm-referenced', in that the scores from a sample of pupils were represented as the population norms. Thus children placed at different points in the score range are compared with their peers or a wider reference group. 'Reading age', for example, purports to locate a pupil as a member of a comparable sub-population of children whose development is at the same age-related stage.

During the last few years there has been increasing interest in two other kinds of test, that is, diagnostic and 'criterion-referenced' tests. Both of these purport to show what a pupil can do in relation to a field of learning. These tests might well be referred to as 'proficiency tests' when the match between what is tested and the curriculum is very close. In a field such as Reading it is not possible to specify every word and phrase in the curriculum because children hopefully will not be con-fined to a single reading scheme or text. However, sub-domains can be specified in whatever detail the test constructor decides. An example of this approach is *Yardsticks* (Milward *et al.*, 1973), a Mathematics test with six levels covering the six to 11 years age range. There are 293 objectives overall written to exemplify the primary mathematics curriculum. The test booklets contain sets of questions for each objective. Teachers can choose when to assess an objective, so there is no pre-scribed order of administration. For the younger age-groups there are five questions for each objective, whilst the older age-groups' tests have ten. Each pupil's question book has a record chart, so progress can readily be checked. Simple rules to relate test results to teaching are suggested, that is, pupils who score 4 or 5 correct (or 8, 9 and 10) per test objective should proceed to new work; those who score 3 (or 6 and 7) should review work related to the objective; and those with lower scores should have remedial help. This test has been described in some detail because it illustrates how the use of results from the test can be related to the test specification. In this instance the test rationale can be readily appreciated.

Not all 'diagnostic' tests are criterion referenced. One normed test which is widely used (*Richmond Tests of Basic Skills*, see Hieronymous, Lindquist and France, 1975) has five major areas which are represented by 11 tests. These are Vocabulary, Reading Comprehension, Spelling, Use of Capital Letters, Punctuation, Map Reading, Graphs and Tables, Use of Reference Materials, Mathematics Concepts and Mathematics Problem-solving. All of the tests are scored by summing the responses, and these raw scores are interpreted through tables of norms which essentially indicate the pupil's standing in relation to the norm group, in this case a population of pupils in the same school year. It is claimed that the normed results provide diagnosis of areas of general strengths and weaknesses.

A different approach to diagnostic assessment is followed in the *Chelsea Diagnostic Mathematics Tests* (Hart *et al.*, 1977–84). There are ten tests: Algebra; Fractions 1; Fractions 2; Graphs; Measurement; Number Operations; Place Value and Decimals; Ratio and Proportion; Reflection and Rotation; and Vectors. Total scores are not recorded, nor are criteria related to 'mastery' levels of performance specified. In these tests each pupil's responses are coded according to patterns established through research to show which errors have been made (if any). Pupils' error patterns are used to indicate in what ways pupils have developed within a field and what aspects need remedial attention to enable further progress to be made.

The procedure by which tests scaled in the same way can be used as a 'battery' has been mentioned. When this is done, it is possible to present the scores as a list or as a string (that is, in a column of figures or in a row). Some test authors have used this kind of result as the basis for so-called profiles. The idea is that separate scores can be compared readily because the scale used is common to all of the tests. Consequently, it is said, *relative* strengths and weaknesses can be identified through inspection of 'the profile'. Given that the necessary statistical questions about score comparisons can be answered satisfactorily (see Chapter 6), there are some possibilities for interpreting diagnostically attainment test profiles.

Test authors have for many years used the concept of 'level' to arrange tests in a successive order, usually matched with age-groups. Hence, levels of this kind are norm-referenced when the scores are used to place pupils relative to each other. Another version of 'level' embodies the idea of complexity, that is, of skills or knowledge which calls for understanding interrelated processes. The TGAT structure merges the two, by referring to the work appropriate to differing age-groups and levels of performance pitched at ascending attainment targets.

Consequently, the 10 levels form an ordinal scale, and though complexity is only weakly defined, it is strongly inferred.

However, there is a sharp contrast between norm-referenced attainment test profiles and tests which examine pupils' operating methods for successful ways of working and error patterns. The norm-referenced profile essentially describes attainment in relation to the average scores from a comparator population. In contrast, the operations tests indicate the concepts and procedures which a pupil can use or needs to learn within a domain. With regard to diagnosis, the norm-referenced profiles give descriptive information, whereas the tests based on functional domains offer causal information. As the diagram earlier in this chapter reminds us (Figure 3.1), all diagnostic test results should be interpreted in the wider contexts of the child's history of attainment and the particular curriculum being studied.

The highly specific nature of causal diagnosis is recognized in computerized tests aimed at analysing the strategies a pupil adopts when attempting basic mathematics operations. Variations in complexity are programmed into a sequence of questions, so that attainment within a domain can be scanned from extremely simple beginnings (for example $1 + 2 = ?$). Correct responses lead rapidly to more complex concepts (for example $3(2 + 7) = ?$) and extensive computation (for example $3.5(2.96 + 8.153) = ?$). The pupil's response, if incorrect, is compared with a large repertoire of characteristic errors. Consistency of error strategies can be tested by having the computer generate replications of the question type which was answered incorrectly. Pinpointing at this level of detail is what an individual tutor might do, given time. The computer has as much time as it takes and – unlike a printed test – a virtually unlimited set of questions.

One requirement which ought to characterize attainment tests of the various kinds described is appropriateness of the content for the pupils for whom the test is designed. Hence the norm-referenced tests should have a curriculum analysis and a specification showing how the parts identified are represented by the items. This point is extremely important when tests are produced for successive age-groups. One purpose claimed for these sets of test is that they provide a means for checking a pupil's progress over several years. Without some means for judging whether the test content reflects the curriculum followed by pupils, this kind of indicator is difficult to interpret. A final point, therefore, is that inspection of the test items is not a sufficient guide as to how the curriculum domain has been defined and sampled. This aspect of defining test contents is discussed in Chapter 7.

This chapter has identified the major areas of testing by reference to various kinds of attribute. For the most part, the distinctions made are fairly clear cut, even though everyday usage tends to treat attainment, ability and achievement as much the same thing. In Chapter 4 we will see that tests cannot be classified as readily, mainly because different features may be present or combined in a large variety of ways.

Multiple assessments

On occasions a survey or inquiry in a school utilizes several tests or assessments. One international study (Lapointe, Mead and Phillips, 1989, and Keys and Foxman, 1989) involved 13 countries or educational territories (French speaking and English speaking provinces in Canada). Each used the same set of tests or questionnaires to illuminate Mathematics and Science attainment comparisons. Both Mathematics and Science samples also answered questionnaires on Opportunity to Learn, Homework, Help with Science at Home, Attitudes to Science, Television Viewing, Homework in Other Subjects, and Exploration and Investigation. For Mathematics the accompanying measures concerned Mathematics Activities in Classrooms, Homework and Attitudes to Mathematics. These broader assessments greatly enriched the interpretation that was possible of the levels of proficiency indicated in different territories.

CHAPTER 4
Test Types

There is really no simple typology of tests. When constructors consider the kinds of test they want to develop, they have a number of options available to them which have to be weighed in relation to the purpose intended for the test, the population it is designed for, and the circumstances expected to govern its administration. Several of these options are sketched out below in the form of contrasting definitions:

Group test
An instrument designed to be administered simultaneously to a set of people by one supervisor.

Individual test
An instrument designed to be administered to one individual at a time.

Objective type
Questions and alternative responses are fixed; only specified responses are marked correct; responses are usually multiple-choice, but other types can be used.

Subjective type
Questions may allow for individuality of interpretation and response. Markers judge answers by reference to a model or according to their view of implicit merit.

Short answer
Single words, phrases or sentences only need to be supplied by the person answering the test.

Extended answer
Paragraphs, essays or a constructed response such as a diagram or computer program have to be supplied as answers to questions.

Diagnostic
Tests designed to indicate aspects of a pupil's performance which are relatively weak, with the intention that once discovered suitable remedial learning can be engendered.

Descriptive
Test scores indicate what a child can do in respect to the field of activity sampled by the test items.

Readiness
Here the test samples prerequisite attributes thought to determine performance on learning tasks yet to come.

Capability
Here the test questions or tasks are chosen to represent as closely as possible a specified activity. In what aspects can the person demonstrate capability or competence?

Norm referenced
Special credence is given to the distribution of scores provided by populations or representative samples, so that all individual scores are interpreted as a rank order relative to all others.

Criterion referenced
A performance criterion is defined and items devised to test whether or not an individual can meet or surpass the standard embodied by the criterion. Hence competence or mastery is shown by giving a minimum number of correct answers.

Convergent
The notion of convergent thinking is applied to item responses, in that only one 'correct' answer is required.

Divergent
In these tests an item stem is designed to prompt a range of answers some of which may be highly idiosyncratic and yet will still be acceptable.

Pencil and paper
All test materials are printed and responses are either written or marked on prepared answer sheets.

Performance
Test materials may be printed or otherwise orally administered, but response requires actions such as speaking, manipulating objects, carrying out a task, playing an instrument or using apparatus.

Standardized
Every aspect of test presentation and completion is specified, as are the questions and acceptable answers.

Interactive
Test presentation may be varied according to a pupil's responses which are not limited to predetermined answers or given procedures.

Computerized/automated
Test instructions and items are administered by computer; responses are made via the computer keyboard, joystick, light-pen or other device; and scoring and statistical transformations are done by the computer, which may print out scores and a prose interpretation.

Invigilated
Test administration is done by people who observe instructions and supervise candidates. Thereafter, scripts may be scored by examiners, by checkers or by optical mark readers (OMR) when answers are of the multiple-choice type.

Categorical
When the test rationale is based on a theory which typifies people, responses can be used to allocate individuals into discrete categories.

Classificatory
Test score distributions are divided at particular points to place respondents into hierarchical levels or to assign grades.

Integrated tasks
A sequence of tasks is
devised aimed at evoking
multi-mode responses from
the pupil; these are assessed
for various components, e.g.
interpreting a drawing, oral
communication, science
observation, practical
mathematics, estimating
linear measure, etc. in
respect of the levels given
in the National Curriculum
attainment target schemes.

Graduated or graded
A test which is scored to
give a sequence of grades;
or a set of tests each
designed to indicate
attainment at a point in a
sequence of stages.

Standard assessment tasks
The TGAT term for test
situations which will be
presented to pupils in a
uniform manner in order to
evoke responses for
appraisal in relation to
certain levels of attainment
target components.

Uni-dimensional attribute
A test with a range of
questions representing
various parts of a domain,
with each devised to assess
an aspect of a single variable
or attribute; e.g. a pupil
might explain verbally how
a problem in mathematics
was tackled, but the
assessment would only refer
to mathematical problem-
solving.

Pass/fail
A test interpreted, so that
any score above a cut-off
point is a pass or below is a
fail.

*Unstandardized or
Idiosyncratic tasks*
When tests are set by
different people for
particular groups of pupils
and the content reflects
features arbitrarily
determined by the tester;
e.g. two or more teachers of
the same curriculum could
each set a test with little
material in common.

Amongst the above distinctions, many people regard the most
important one as norm vs criterion referencing. Norms are
explained more fully in Chapter 5. Criterion-referencing

aspects have been alluded to and are discussed more fully in Chapter 7.

The complexity of the testing field is exemplified by the American at a conference who defined the ideal test of mathematics for his city authority. It would be, he said, 'A locally specified, criterion-referenced, fully objective, standardized, diagnostic group test of competence'. This man's main purpose was to discover which pupils had mastered the prescribed local curriculum. His secondary purpose was to uncover the difficulties being experienced by the so-called non-masters.

The test description was challenged by someone in the conference session who asked how it was possible to have a criterion-referenced test which is standardized; the two features were mistakenly viewed as incompatible. The problem encapsulated in this instance is the definition of the testing outcome (diagnostic/competence), which is a function of the score or categorization awarded to the individual pupil.

The labels used to type tests can be distinctly unhelpful to the user. The best advice one can give is to be critical. For example, a test which is presented as suitable for gauging a primary school pupil's knowledge and skills on transfer to secondary school is plainly inadequate if there are too few items to enable satisfactory sampling of the curriculum. The description for such a test might be given as: a group test of 50 items, objective with multiple-choice machine-scored answer sheets, normed for a population of pupils aged from 10 years 9 months to 11 years 9 months, with pencil and paper presentation, standardized and criterion referenced through a recording sheet keyed to the item contents.

This description is quite acceptable, and tests of this type have been developed in the USA by reputable publishers. However, the test might be criticized on a number of counts. One is that the items do not match the local curriculum which the pupils transferring to secondary school have had. Another is that the representation of the curriculum is too thin, for instance, a test of 50 mathematics items will have no more than one or two questions representing the topics which make up the curriculum. A further objection would arise (to multiple-choice response format) if it is important for children to demonstrate their working methods. Taking these points together, a better test would be one with subjective-type items marked according to guidelines by teachers who understand them; also the test should be long enough to contain an adequate sample of items for each recognized curriculum domain. The test might then be stipulated as: standardized, criteria-referenced, group, pencil and paper subjective-type items, scored to indicate a profile of a pupil's capabilities.

Nowadays it is possible for a user to specify the sort of test required and then compile trial versions from banks of items. The advantage to the user is that test characteristics can be selected to suit a procedure designed to enable pupils' results to be used effectively. This is opposite to the way most tests are chosen, by someone scanning catalogues and then obtaining specimen copies which are appraised for suitability. The disadvantage is that item banks are expensive to create and utilization demands specialist services. Even so, a sizeable number of LEAs are commissioning bank-built tests which reflect the curriculum guidelines or suit a prescribed purpose.

The bulk of published test material is of the pencil and paper type. Even tests which employ tape recorded sound for the communication mode make use of printed answer sheets. The consequence is that far too few test situations call for an original response from the pupil. In this respect teachers' own tests or other types of assessment could employ speaking, writing, drawing or other *expressive* kinds of performance. This is especially important in many areas of study in order to represent the curriculum properly, and to convey the message that productive and creative work is highly valued.

The type of testing carried out by schools carries many overtones. Assessment takes place in social settings and the results have social consequences; those who control the assessing are the ones whose values count. When results are used, however sensitively, to judge the work of teachers or authorities, the inherent characteristics of the assessment device acquire implicit meanings. Hence, if pupils were judged from their responses to tests with multiple-choice questions and nothing else, it is fairly certain that the generation and expression of ideas through writing would greatly diminish. The teacher who persisted with setting and marking essays, observations of problem-solving and verbal accounts of activities would be left in little doubt that multiple-choice tests should be used predominantly, especially if the pupils did badly at them. In this context, the TGAT members should be commended by the teaching profession for their rejection of tests or tasks which did not reflect activities in the curriculum, and for their insistence on the importance of teachers' assessments based on observations.

An author of a test ought to justify the choice of test type by illustrating (in the test manual) how it is suited to particular uses. For example, a test of 'reading readiness' should give the score bands for three kinds of pupil: (1) those who are 'ready', (2) those who are 'not ready' and (3) those in the border zone between the two recognized stages. There is no point whatever in producing population norms for this type of test, as the matter it deals with is not whether a pupil is more or less average, but whether a child should have a pre-reading curriculum or is to start or continue with learning to read.

Test authors cannot of course address every intention and circumstance. Users have the responsibility for analysing for themselves whether a test of a particular type, with specific features, is capable of meeting purposes they anticipate. The three critical questions to be answered are:

(a) how will the results be used to inform judgements and make decisions?
(b) what type of test or other form of assessment will produce the required results?
(c) what materials and procedures will be needed to administer the test and to obtain pupils' results and any derived information?

These are *design* questions. They call for the exercise of design skills, particularly those of modelling. Of course modelling cannot be done without imagination or knowledge of materials and techniques.

An illustration of an enterprise which would have benefited from modelling comes from an LEA which wished to keep track of each pupil's reading development over the primary years. Hence it was decided to supply schools with tests to be given annually towards the end of the summer term. The type of test required to meet this purpose seemed commonplace enough; i.e. standardized group tests of reading. In the event, a huge amount of data in the form of lists of pupils' results school by school was accumulated over a seven-year period. For the early years there were reading ages, for the remaining ones there was a mixture of norm-referenced scores and reading level indices (see Fry, 1968, for example). The sheer amount of data and lack of compatibility was such that comparisons between years were not carried out, so it was not possible to show whether children given remedial support had progressed into the middling range of attainment and, conversely, whether pupils whose early reading was satisfactory had dropped back. The basic problem with this design was that the type of test had been under-specified. Also though the administration had worked extremely well, gathering and entering the individual pupils' results from schools had fallen behind because ways for handling the year-on-year data had not been devised or clerical help provided.

Practically all design problems have alternative solutions which offer different advantages. For this reason it is important that different types of test are examined and designs for their use compared. The process of laying out test result applications is dealt with in Chapter 9. However, before considering how to approach the satisfactory use of tests, it is necessary to know something about the kinds of scales used for expressing pupils' performance, and to consider methods for handling the resultant data.

CHAPTER 5
Scales and their Interpretation

This chapter deals with the types of scale which are used to express pupils' test performance. The statistical basis of the various scales is described, so that the reader can appreciate the underlying concepts. Because some fundamental ideas are involved, such as a measured *variable*, its central point and dispersion, a limited use of statistical notation has been introduced. The reader may find that an electronic calculator will be useful as understanding the concepts is often helped by carrying out the simple computations involved.

Raw scores

The total figure obtained by adding up the values awarded for each correct response to test questions is known as the 'raw score'. Clearly, a figure on its own is of little consequence; it is necessary to know at least what was the maximum possible score.

Under certain conditions the pupil's raw score in relation to the maximum for the test might provide enough information for sensible interpretation. For example, a raw score of 24 on a criterion-referenced test with a maximum score of 25 can be confidently accepted as showing almost complete knowledge of, or competence at, the domain tested. However, a more complete understanding can be obtained when other raw score data is available. For instance, if the score of 24 was obtained by only one pupil out of 160 tested, and the next best score was 17, the individual with 24 points would be regarded as exceptional in terms of the test coverage. Other pertinent data might be the *range* of scores, that is, from the lowest score obtained to the highest, say, 15 to 24, a range of 9 points, and an indication of the central score point. A slight difficulty here, however, is that there are several different methods for determining the centre of a distribution of pupils' scores, and these are commonly referred to as *measures of central tendency*.

The most common measure of central tendency is the average for the group tested. Introducing some notation, in which any pupils' score is denoted by x and the number tested is denoted by n, the total for the group as a whole is Σx, where Σ stands for 'the sum of'; the average or *mean* (to use the statistical term) is $\dfrac{\Sigma x}{n}$.

Two other measures of central tendency are the *mode* and the *median*. The modal score is the one obtained by most people among the group tested. In the example given below the number of pupils with a score of 17 exceeds the number who obtained any other score in the range, so the mode is 17.

The median is slightly more complicated to explain. Essentially it is the score obtained by the person at the mid-point of the rank order. With 160 pupils in a group, the mid-point is occupied jointly by the 80th and 81st pupil; as illustrated by the imaginary distribution:

raw score	no. obtaining score	
25	0	
24	1	
23	0	
22	0	
21	0	
20	0	
19	0	
18	0	
17	73	
16	40	← 80th person is in
15	46	this score group
14 or below	0	
	n = 160	

In this example there would be little point in calculating the median because the majority of the pupils would be tightly bunched into groups scoring 17, 16 and 15. However, this distribution can be used to show how to deal with a number of ties (that is, more than one person with the same score). First, the score scale is treated as a number line, hence 16 is the integer between 15.5 and 16.5. This unit of score is allocated in even bits to each of the pupils with a score of 16, so hypothetically each of these can be ranked using increments of 1/40. Working from the lowest rank upwards, 46 pupils scored 15, so there are (80 − 46) pupils to count in order to reach the 80th individual, that is, 34. (*Check*: 46 + 34 = 80.) So (34 × 1/40) is the fraction required to locate the 80th pupil up the score scale from 15.5. The value of this fraction is 0.85, hence the 80th person is assumed to have a score of 15.5 + 0.85, that is, 16.35.

This short exercise with measures of central tendency can be completed by calculating the arithmetic mean for the distribution of raw scores. The total number of marks (Σx) is readily calculated: 1 pupil with 24 is 24 points; 73 with 17 is 1241 points; 40 with 16 is 640 points; and 46 with 15 is 690 points. The total comes to 2595; averaged over 160 pupils gives 16.22 points per pupil. This is the value of the mean

$$\frac{\Sigma x}{n}$$

which is denoted as $\bar{x}$.

We can now see that the three measures are fairly close in this example, i.e. mode 17, median, 16.35 and mean 16.22.

Test scores for groups can be examined in relation to distributions of raw scores and, in particular, a central tendency measure. For example, an LEA education committee had the tests used in a survey with nine-year-olds issued at a feedback meeting. They were able to appreciate the reading attainment of pupils more fully when it was pointed out that the middle-scoring pupils (those near the median) would probably have answered correctly the first 23 out of the 44 items in the test (in which the items were broadly graded for complexity). They were also quite impressed by the variety of the items and by the finding that around half of the children knew the answer to; 'He saw the job . . . in the local paper and applied for it.' In this instance the central tendency measure was related to a pupil attribute of abiding interest.

Both group results from tests and a single pupil's score can be interpreted as measures of a *variable*. This general term is used in two ways: (1) to define the attribute in respect of which individuals vary (for example, the concept of attitude towards enjoyment of Science activities); and (2) more precisely, to define a metric for the attribute. Users need to have knowledge of the variable, in both senses, to interpret a pupil's score properly.

As a minimum, a measure of a variable is given by its central point and associated dispersion relative to that point. For the mode the appropriate measure of dispersion is the range, and for the median an appropriate indicator of dispersion is the difference on the scale which separates the 25th and 75th individuals in a list of 100; in other words, the 25th and 75th percentile positions, for example, in a class of 28 pupils the scores of the 7th and 21st pupils would give the data required. (*Note*: these are taken in ascending order, higher percentile ranks go with higher scores.)

When the mean is calculated, one measure of dispersion which is occasionally used is the *average deviation*. This is the average of the differences between each individual's score and the mean.

Clearly, if all of the differences above the mean were added up, they would be equal to all of the differences below the mean added up, and taking positive and negative differences together the total sum would be zero. When the signs are ignored and the differences for every pupil in a distribution summed and divided by the number in the group, the result is the average of the deviations. The notation for the difference between any pupil's score, x, and the group mean, $\bar{x}$, can be written as $(x - \bar{x})$. As pointed out above, the algebraic sum of these (i.e. taking the sign of the difference into account) must come to zero. For example, for 20 pupils with raw scores distributed, as shown below, the deviations from the mean for each score are given in the last column. As the figures show, the total number of points is 480, and for 20 pupils this gives a mean score of 24:

raw score scale	no. of pupils	points per score group	differences per score group	total of deviations
30	1	30	6 × 1 =	+6
29	0	0	5 × 0 =	0
28	2	56	4 × 2 =	+8
27	2	54	3 × 2 =	+6
26	0	0	2 × 0 =	0
25	1	25	1 × 1 =	+1
24	5	120	0 × 5 =	0
23	6	138	−1 × 6 =	−6
22	0	0	−2 × 0 =	0
21	1	21	−3 × 1 =	−3
20	1	20	−4 × 1 =	−4
19	0	0	−5 × 0 =	0
18	0	0	−6 × 0 =	0
17	0	0	−7 × 0 =	0
16	1	16	−8 × 1 =	−8
	n = 20	$\Sigma x = 480$		$\Sigma(x - \bar{x}) = 0$

$$\bar{x} = \frac{\Sigma x}{n} = \frac{480}{20} = 24$$

In this tidy example, then, the total deviation, when signs are disregarded, is 42. This could be averaged for the 20 pupils to give 2.1 points. Hence we could say that the average deviation on either side of the mean of 24 is 2.1 points.

A more widely used index of dispersion is the *standard deviation* (SD). There is a statistical reason why the standard deviation is preferred, as will become apparent. The SD is calculated by squaring the difference from the mean for each pupil, adding the sum of these squares, averaging the squares' total and then finding the square root of the average. In squaring the deviations all of the signs take positive values, as shown below with values taken from the previous data.

raw score scale	$(x - \bar{x})$	$(x - \bar{x})^2$	no. of pupils in score group	squared values per score group
30	+6	36	1	36
29	+5	25	0	0
28	+4	16	2	32
27	+3	9	2	18
26	+2	4	0	0
25	+1	1	1	1
24	0	0	5	0
23	−1	1	6	6
22	−2	4	0	0
21	−3	9	1	9
20	−4	16	1	16
19	−5	25	0	0
18	−6	36	0	0
17	−7	49	0	0
16	−8	64	1	64

$$\Sigma(x - \bar{x})^2 = 182$$
(sum of squares)

$$\frac{\Sigma(x - \bar{x})^2}{n} = \frac{182}{20} = 9.1 \qquad \text{(mean square)}$$

$$\sqrt{\left[\frac{\Sigma(x - \bar{x})^2}{n} \right]} = \sqrt{9.1} = 3.017 \quad \text{(SD)}$$

From the raw score data the various measures of dispersion are as follows: *range*, 30 − 16 = 14 points; *inter-quartile range*, 25th to 75th percentile, that is, 5th to 15th pupil up the distribution, is 22.5 + 0.33 to 25, that is, 22.85 to 25, a difference of 2.15 points; *average deviation*, 2.1 points; and *standard deviation*, 3.02 points.

With the appropriate measure of central tendency representing the mid-point of the distribution, the raw score summary for the variable measured by the test is:

mode 23	range 14 points
median 23.7	inter-quartile range 2.15 points
mean 24	standard deviation 3.02 points

Of course, with an electronic calculator with functions for square roots, or for mean and SD, the calculations are easily done.

The main point of the worked example is to show how a measure of central tendency and dispersion convey information which improves score interpretation. For example, a score of 23 or 24 represents average performance, whilst 26 or better lies in the highest quarter of the range and 21 or lower lies in the lowest quarter. If the test was referenced to a given domain (for example, a course specification with questions sampling each element), the maximum score possible becomes important, as does a zero score. In the case illustrated, no one scored less than 16 points, indicating that no less than 16 aspects of the domain had been understood by everyone in the group tested. Views about how much of the domain had been understood by the group would depend on whether the maximum score was 30 or set at a higher point. Obviously a teacher who was assessing his/her pupils' understanding of a unit of curriculum would be pleased had the maximum raw score been 30, and might have been dismayed had it been 100.

Interpretation of raw scores can also be assisted by showing the distribution graphically. Two representations are given in Figure 5.1, one with each score group separate and the other with score groups amalgamated into threes and with a perpendicular score axis.

Figure 5.1: **Graphical representations of a raw score distribution**

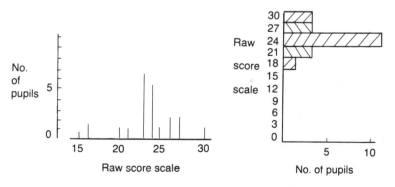

The usual convention is to have the scale along the horizontal axis and the number of pupils counted vertically. Whichever way the axes are arranged, the result is a graph of the *frequency distribution*. This is the kind of distribution referred to in the TGAT report, for representing the numbers of pupils in any group tested towards the end of a key stage (that is, 5–7 years, 7 to 11 years, 11 to 14 years, 14 to 16 years) who are assessed as attaining each of the levels available for the curriculum components evaluated.

The importance of raw scores is played down or overlooked in many test manuals, especially when other scales are used; however, as the connection between the test rationale and interpretation stems from the raw score distribution, it is advisable to pay attention to it.

Percentages

Most of us are familiar with the concept that a test score can be transformed to another equivalent score scale to assist with its interpretation. For this reason the everyday practice of taking a score and expressing it as a percentage of the maximum possible value is widely accepted. The simplicity of this method of *standardization* arises from the linearity of the relationship between the original scale and its equivalent. This can be illustrated with two number lines, as shown below:

Raw score scale   0 _____ $\frac{x}{2}$ _____ x (Max)

Percentage scale   0 _____ 50 _____ 100

The formula to go from any score x to a percentage score is:

$$\frac{x}{x(\text{Max})} \times 100 = P\%$$

For example, 8 out of 40 is transformed as follows:

$$\frac{8}{40} \times 100 = 20\%$$

Conversely, the formula for finding the raw score from a percentage is:

$$\frac{P}{100} \times x(Max) = x$$

For example:

$$\frac{20}{100} \times 40 = 8$$

It is useful to speculate about the meanings commonly attached to percentages. For example, 50 per cent in an examination usually results in a 'pass'. It seems to denote too that the candidate knew about half of the curriculum dealt with in an examination paper. Also 100 per cent shows that there is an absolute upper limit to performance, whilst 0 per cent sets an absolute lower limit. Hence, anyone who was awarded 0 per cent would be seen as knowing nothing about the domain examined. Other vague understandings about percentages are that 65–75 per cent is quite a good standard; 25–35 per cent is really quite poor; 60 per cent is two times better than 30 per cent, etc.

This latter point is quite intriguing as this relationship can only hold good up to 100 per cent; so what is twice as good a result as 51 per cent? Another widely held idea is that percents can be averaged over two or more results, for example, in a two-part examination with each part carrying equal weight. These comments show that the percentages scale is widely accepted because we believe we understand it. In fact averaging entails adding and dividing the percentage units, thus treating the scale as a ratio scale, whereas the raw score units are aggregated as an interval scale. Furthermore, the dispersion of scores for each variable affects the weighting achieved when pupils' scores on two tests are combined (see Chapter 6).

For many criterion-referenced tests, especially those which have a structure built round learning objectives, changing raw scores to percentage marks would obscure the results. But for indicating a performance level relative to implied upper and lower limits of performance, percentages are useful as a standard scale. Percentages should not be used without careful thought, and one pitfall to be avoided is to transform short raw score scales. When this is done, one raw score point difference becomes a large increment as a percentage, a fact which tends to be overlooked when comparisons between individuals are made.

Age-equivalent scales

The most well-known version of this type of scale is 'reading age', but others such as 'mental age' have been used for some tests. One method of determining age-equivalent scores is to calculate the mean raw score for each of several specified age-groups. When the age-groups are successive and the means rise progressively, the results are very convincing. The logic in this case is to accept a pupil's score as indicating performance on a par with that of the age-group associated with a particular mean score. For example, the mean raw scores for a mathematics test of 40 items might be:

age-group (years/months)	8/0	8/3	8/6	8/9	9/0	9/3	9/6	9/9	10/0
mean score	10	14	19	20	22	27	28	29	34

A pupil with a score of 24 would then be allocated an age-equivalent score, by interpolation, of 9 years 1 month.

The other method for determining age equivalents is to administer trial tests to samples of pupils in different age-groups and then to identify items which are passed (or failed) by half of each group. These items then make up the published test. This method was used for some of the single-word reading tests. The interpretation of results from these is that the highest point (that is, word) reached successfully by a child represents the average attainment of the age-group which corresponds to that point in the test. When each year-group was divided into 12 sub-groups, the 12 words for the year were supposed to represent the median attainment of each monthly sub-population. From the scaling point of view this method is interesting because a pupil's total score is not required; progress through the test up to the point of failure is equated directly with performance, of average pupils of a particular age.

The appropriateness of age-equivalent scores has been questioned critically (Guilford, 1965; Cronbach, 1970) and, more recently, in respect of reading age by Vincent and Cresswell (1976). Two of the objections to this type of scale are the spurious degree of accuracy which the age equivalent conveys, and the lack of information about age-equivalent score distributions for particular populations. The validity of the first objection can be appreciated when it is realized that most children do not abruptly reach a failure point in a test with graded items as if they have encountered an insuperable obstacle. Quite the reverse, in most cases pupils fail one or two items, succeed at several more, fail a few, pass one or two and then continue to fail though perhaps with the occasional success. So the tester has to apply a scoring rule of some kind to make a decision about age equivalence. The consequence is that a seemingly exact measure (of attribute age) is being adduced from an approximate measure. Even worse, the implications of any chronological age vs attribute age discrepancy cannot be evaluated properly. Worse still, seemingly accurate quotients derived by making a fraction from attribute age and chronological age multiplied by 100 are used to indicate whether or not performance at the attribute is in line with expectation.

Of course older children in wide age-range populations generally perform better at a test than younger ones, but their experience and thinking processes are very different too. So the significance of so-called retardation is quite different at various ages, particularly because the development of attributes such as inferential reading does not advance in regular increments as does age.

Teachers who prefer to continue with age-equivalent assessments, particularly of reading, are invited to look in the test manuals for any information on the standard error of the reading ages as determined by the test (the standard error concept comes later, in Chapter 6); the proportion of children in a given age sub-population who were 6 months, 12 months, 18 months, 24 months, etc., either retarded or advanced; and any interpretations of the reading attainment characteristics ascribed to the various age equivalents and discrepancies. Hopefully the lack of information will encourage them to relinquish age-equivalent scales both as a concept and as a measure of development.

Centiles

Sometimes referred to as 'percentiles', this scale is based on the division of the population into 100 equal parts. The lowest-scoring hundredth obtain total raw scores within a certain range at the lowest end of the distribution – and so on for successive hundredths. For example, the 23rd centile is the point in the raw score scale which marks the upper end of the range spanned by the lowest-scoring 23 per cent of the population. It follows that the same point is at the lowest end of the range which contains the highest-scoring 77 per cent. The centile points given in some test manuals should be estimated from the results obtained from substantial population samples.

The method for determining centiles resembles that for calculating the median, described earlier. However, as division into hundredths gives precision that is usually not warranted, it is sometimes considered adequate to express the scale as tenths, called *deciles*. For example, the 7th decile is the range of scores between the points which divide the lowest sixth-tenths of the population from the upper two-tenths. A pupil scoring in this range would be said to have come within the 7th decile (this would include all of the centiles from 70 to 79).

It is worth noting that centiles and deciles are primarily rank-order scales for comparing a pupil's performance within a relevant population, and in this sense they are normative. The raw score ranges for each decile will usually not be equal.

Also when the overall score distribution on a test is found to be tightly bunched, there will be little real difference in the attribute assessed between adjacent deciles; and the converse applies when the raw score distribution turns out to be widely dispersed. For these and other reasons concerned with the validity of the measure, it is advisable to study closely any information in the test manual on the raw score distributions obtained by the sample(s) from which the norms were obtained.

Standardized scores

Any number of procedures for standardizing raw scores can be devised, and the percentage conversion described previously is just one method with which we are all familiar. However, when the term *standardized score* is used in testing it has a particular meaning, in that the basis for the conversion is the deviation from the mean. Accordingly, data from a sample of pupils is used to calculate *deviation units*. The standard deviation is regarded as the basic unit, and the scale is laid out on either side of the mean. When the SD is one unit of measurement and the mean ($\bar{x}$) is assigned a value of zero, the scale line picture is as follows:

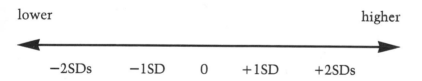

lower   higher

-2SDs -1SD   0 $+1$SD $+2$SDs

We have to bear in mind that the SD is a form of average which represents the dispersion of groups of pupils at different raw score points in relation to the mean. The raw score distribution is unlikely to be symmetrical or even, as the diagrams in Figure 5.2 indicate.

When this form of standardization is adopted, a pupil's score is expressed as a proportion of an SD above or below the mean.

Figure 5.2:   Illustration of asymmetrical raw score distributions

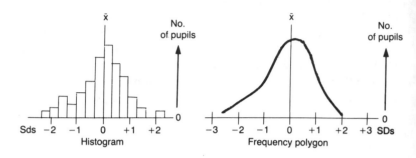

For instance, suppose a test had 100 items each carrying one mark, and also that the mean for a representative sample of pupils came to 61.3 and the SD was 8.7, then anyone with a score of 61.3 + 8.7 would have a deviation score of +1, that is, a total of 70 would be equivalent to +1. Similarly, a score of 45 would have a deviation score value of $(45 - 61.3)/8.7 = -1.84$ units.

It is customary to use z as the symbol for deviation units. As a formula, this reads $(x - \bar{x})/SD = z$ units of deviation.

It is very rare for z to have a value greater than five. So with a scale range of $\bar{x}$ plus and minus 5 SDs (that is, five deviation units on either side of the mean) the negative values can be eliminated by adding 5 to every deviation unit. This merely changes the scale to one with a lowest value of 0 to a highest value of 10. In fact the constant used to eliminate the inconvenience of negative signs is chosen arbitrarily, any value that is sensible will do. With the values given above, -1.84 converts to 3.16 deviation units on a scale with a mean of 5 and an SD of 1.

A further transformation can be done by giving the deviation units any scale equivalent which is suitable. A common multiple is 10. Combined with the value of 5 used to transpose the mean point to a more convenient value, the mean is fixed at a scale point of 50. Hence 3.16 becomes 31.6 on a deviation scale with a mean of 50 and an SD of 10. This particular scale is very useful for re-scaling school examination marks to bring them to a common metric for interpretation or for combining (if two raw scores are added together when a group has taken two papers or exams, the set of scores which has the largest dispersion carries more weight; using the same SD gives equal weights or provides a correct basis for arbitrary differential weights; and school computers could handle the arithmetic with ease).

Figure 5.3: Skewed distribution changed to normal distribution

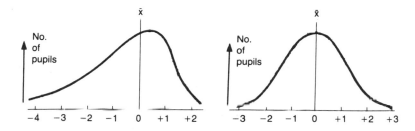

Standardization using the deviation unit as the basis can be taken to another dimension by adjusting the raw score distribution to fit the normal probability curve. Imagine a cross section through a lop-sided jelly, as shown in Figure 5.3; then imagine that it has been gently pushed to become symmetrical with the bulk piled up towards the middle and the remainder spread towards the sides. Clearly in a frequency distribution changes which balance the shape could be achieved by shrinking the raw score units under the slope to the left of the first curve and stretching some of those to the right (see Figure 5.4).

This model, the normal curve, is used because it has features which assist with the interpretation of test scores. The principal feature is that the proportions of a population which fall under parts of the curve are known. These proportions are shown in the diagram in Figure 5.5 when the baseline is marked off in three ways: (a) in SD units with a mean of zero; (b) with the SD assigned 10 units and mean fixed at 50; and (c) with the SD assigned 15 units and mean fixed at 100.

It can be seen from the diagram in Figure 5.5 that converting from one normalized scale to another is a very simple

Figure 5.4:   Changes to original scale points due to normalizing distribution

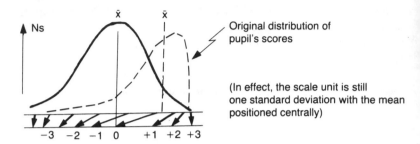

operation. Scale (b) is a normalized form of the deviation scale described previously; it has been used by a few test authors because the results fit within the range of scores available when percentages are used. However, the predominant convention in psychological and educational testing is scale (c).

This graph of the normal distribution shows, for example, that 50 + 34.13 = 84.13 per cent of a population will be assigned to the score range up to and including 115. It is also

Figure 5.5:   Proportions under normal curve

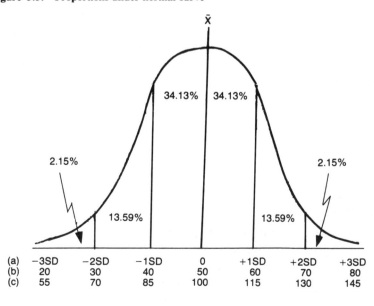

interesting to know, too, that only 26 cases in 10,000 would be expected beyond ±3SD, that is, below a standardized score of 55 or above one of 145; and also, that the highest 1 per cent of the population would be expected to have scores above 135 on this scale.

There are several misunderstandings associated with standardization adjusted to fit the normal curve. A pervasive one is that human attributes are distributed amongst populations 'normally', that is, according to the curve. In fact the raw score distributions on some attribute measures obtained from very carefully drawn large representative samples approach the normal curve shape. There may be, however, features in the measures themselves which contribute to the way in which the sample is divided. For example, most tests of an ability are composed of questions which are graded for 'difficulty' on the basis of trials. The consequence is that when a year group of pupils is tested, there is a hump in the distribution which represents the preponderance of middling performers. If measures of certain other attributes were used, the distributions would be very different. For example, when a test of competence at handling money in everyday situations was given to slower learning children in special schools and children in ordinary schools, the scores were comparable and the distributions in both cases were J-shaped, as shown in Figure 5.6. In this case *the norm* is that most pupils can use money competently. Had the test involved transactions in a foreign language, such as paying for an ice-cream with francs, no doubt the distribution would show a different sort of curve, probably a bi-modal (two humps) shape.

The confusion between a norm and the normal distribution is understandable, especially as the two are often combined in test manuals which have tables of norms for standardized normal scores. It should be kept in mind that a norm essentially describes a social situation, for example, the finding that the majority of children can handle money competently in everyday situations might be expressed by stating that a score of 62 points or over on a 70-item test of handling money was obtained by 85 per cent of the sample. There is no particular significance in the score obtained by 50% of the sample or population. The *norms* for such a test would be given by listing

Figure 5.6:   Example of a non-normal 'natural' distribution

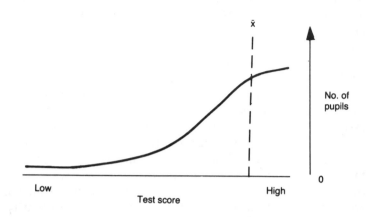

the score levels obtained by successive proportions of the sample.

Test manuals which give scores on the conventional standardized scale may also tabulate the score points which approximate the centile divisions. If not, interpretation is aided by reference to tables relating standardized normal scores to centiles. Table 5.1 is given for intervals of 5 points and shows the expected proportions rounded to the nearest whole number, except at the extremes of the range when rounding is to the nearest 0.5. The first column gives the SD, the second shows the standardized normal scale, the third shows the proportion of the population up to and including a given score and the fourth shows the proportion expected within a score interval – for example, the interval between 105 and 110 points includes 12 per cent of the population.

The last column in the table is by far the most important for interpreting standardized normal scores in terms of population norms. It can be seen that just over a quarter of the population would be expected to score within 5 points of the mean score of 100; also that a half of the population would score within 10 points of the mean, that is, with scores from 90 up to 110. This score bracket can be used to define in a crude way the notion of an average or middling pupil, in itself not a particularly useful concept. But it helps a little with the question:

'what is an exceptional pupil?' We would probably argue against taking the upper and lower quartiles of the distribution and settle for a narrower band, perhaps 9 per cent or maybe 5 per cent. At the upper end these occur above score points of 120 and 125 respectively, and at the lower end the score points are 80 and 75 respectively.

Table 5.1: **Proportions expected within standardized normal score intervals of five points**

Unit SD	Standardized normal scale point	Percentage of population	Proportion within intervals (%)	Quartiles	
				1	
2.33	135	99	1.5		25
2.00	130	97.5	2.5		
1.66	125	95	4.0	24	
1.33	120	91	7.0		
1.00	115	84	9.0		
0.66	110	75	12.0		
0.33	105	63	13.0	26	50
0.00	100	50	13.0		
−0.33	95	37	12.0		
−0.66	90	25	9.0		
−1.00	85	16	7.0		
−1.33	80	9	4.0	24	
−1.66	75	5	2.5		25
−2.00	70	2.5	1.5		
−2.33	65	1		1	

This discussion is not irrelevant in view of the interest in pupils deemed to be unusually able and those with learning difficulties, inevitably commented on in the HMI published reports on schools. Of course any levels chosen are arbitrary and identification with a view to providing for special needs should depend upon a wide range of evidence, test scores included. A further point is that few pupils would be identified as exceptional on one attribute alone and it would, therefore, be preferable to appraise the pupils in a school from a number of standpoints rather than rely upon a single indicator such as a test of reasoning ability.

A crucial factor in the interpretation of standardized normal scores is the quality of the norming data. Little reliance can be placed on norms based on inadequate samples. Hence the test manual has to be examined for detail with respect to sample representativeness (ideally every pupil in a population could have been chosen as a member), sample size (3600 is considered adequate for a sample from a year cohort) and age of data (population changes mean that norms lose currency gradually, so that after ten years or so they can be used only tentatively).

In many test manuals standard normal scores for the conventional scale with a mean of 100 and SD of 15 are expressed as equivalent centile (or percentile) points. Table 5.2 shows that the score of 100 does not divide the distribution into two equal halves, as might be expected. This is because the scores, notionally, are points on a continuous scoreline. So, for example, 100 is the integer corresponding to an interval of 99.5 to 100.5. Accordingly scores of 100 are obtained by a group of individuals. When these are added to all of the other groups with scores below 100, the proportion of the population comes to 51.3. Bearing in mind that the standard normal scores are transformations from unit raw scores, and that any score has a probability of error, pupils' centile positions should be taken as approximate, for example, a pupil with a score of 80 would be at or near the 10th centile.

Standardized age scores

When a variable is found to be influenced by age, it is useful on occasions to have scales which incorporate age allowances. Age effects can be detected quite readily by organizing the scores for different age-groups into separate distributions. Hence if 3600 pupils from one year cohort are sampled, there will be about 300 in each month. If there is an age effect, it will show most clearly in the means for each month group. For example, if a September eight-year-old's sample is tested in February, the youngest member would be 8 years 6 months and the oldest would be almost 9 years 5 months. If the mean test raw score is found to rise gradually across the month groups, there is a cross-sectional age effect. A difference of, say, 6 raw score points across the 12 months means that the

Table 5.2: **Table for converting standardized scores to percentiles**

Standardized score	Percentile	Standardized score	Percentile	Standardized score	Percentile
140	99.7	115	84.9	91	28.5
139	99.6	114	83.3	90	26.3
138	99.5	113	81.6	89	24.2
137	99.4	112	79.7	88	22.2
136	99.3	111	77.8	87	20.3
135	99.1	110	75.0	86	18.4
134	98.9	109	73.7	85	16.7
133	98.7	108	71.5	84	15.1
132	98.5	107	69.1	83	13.6
131	98.2	106	66.7	82	12.2
130	97.9	105	64.3	81	10.9
129	97.5	104	61.8	80	9.7
128	97.1	103	59.2	79	8.6
127	96.7	102	56.6	78	7.6
126	96.1	101	54.0	77	6.7
125	95.5	100	51.3	76	5.9
124	94.9	99	48.7	75	5.1
123	94.1	98	46.0	74	4.5
122	93.3	97	43.4	73	3.9
121	92.4	96	40.8	72	3.3
120	91.4	95	38.2	71	2.9
119	90.3	94	35.7	70	2.5
118	89.1	93	33.3		
117	87.8	92	30.9		
116	86.4				

older pupils as a group have had an advantage. This is nullified by setting the standardized mean for each month group to 100 and normalizing the raw score distributions for each month group.

The result is that differences between pupils' standardized scores due to age are controlled, thus enabling the results for pupils tested at the same time to be compared. Usually the test manual has tables for standardized age score. Often these are printed in month by month columns, but there are some tests with scores for three-monthly groups and others where the user is advised to add a given constant to *younger* pupils' scores when converting raw scores to standardized ones.

The adjustments described above do not take into account the tendency for all pupils to obtain higher scores on a test if it is taken later rather than earlier in their lives. Strictly speaking, test authors or publishers should carry out one or more cross-sectional standardizations at different times of the year if their tests are likely to be used at various times. For example, tests standardized at about the middle of each term will have adequate information on both cross-sectional and longitudinal age variations for reasonably accurate age adjustments to be given.

However, it has to be said that the fine corrections to standardized scores often given in test tables convey an impression of accuracy which is quite unwarranted. There are also difficulties when a test is given to a run of year-groups. These will usually attain progressively higher mean scores. At the same time, there may well be large proportions of pupils within the extreme year-groups who obtain either very high or very low scores. These raw score distributions will be skewed, as shown in Figure 5.7. In addition, the year-groups in the middle of the range will tend to be compressed into a narrow raw score range.

Scores for year-groups A – D

Normalization of each of these distributions will change the shape of groups A and D more than for groups B and C. Consequently, the age compensation is uneven within year-groups. One effect is that children with adjacent raw scores who are a few months different in age can be allocated markedly different standardized scores. This result is highly unsatisfactory as it is an artefact of the statistical procedures. It would be preferable to use a test specifically designed for the age-group concerned. Test users are advised to inspect the standardized age

Figure 5.7: **Raw score distributions for successive age-groups given a single test**

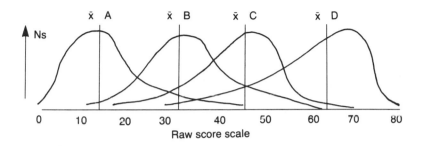

score tables for wide-range tests to see whether the effects described above are apparent. If they are, then the test should not be used for pupils in the age-groups affected.

Stanines and Stens

These are divisions of the standardized normal scale chosen to indicate a pupil's approximate position in a population in a readily interpreted way. Both of these scales have a base unit of one half of a standard deviation. The main difference is that one scale has a middle unit which spans the mean; the other scale has a mid-point, at the mean, which separates two units.

The labels for these scales are contractions of 'standard nines' and 'standard tens' respectively. As the tails of a normal distribution stretch towards infinity the extreme divisions on both scales are not true 'units', as indicated in Figure 5.8 and Table 5.3.

The Stanine scale is quite widely used for reporting test results. Its interpretation should be normative; for instance, a pupil in the third Stanine is one whose test performance placed him/her among the 12.1 per cent whose results were better than the lowest 10.6 per cent of the population. Stens are less widely used. Compared with Stanines, the scale gives more discrimination at the extremes but a disadvantage is that the pupils in the middle range of the distribution are not identified as clearly.

Figure 5.8:   **(a) Stanines in relation to the normal distribution, (b) Stens in relation to the normal distribution**

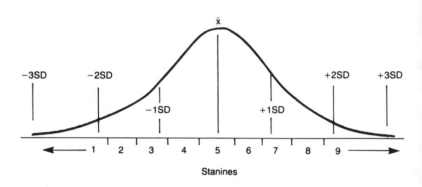

Stanines

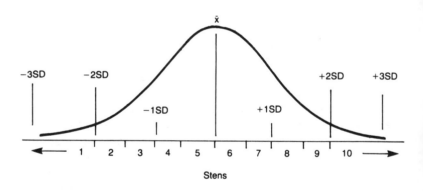

Stens

One justification for using these scales is the approximate nature of test raw scores and standardized normal scores which, like all other measurements, have a degree of error, as discussed in Chapter 6. In fact, the same point applies to classification into Stanines and Stens. Hence some pupils whose performance warrants a Sten of 8 might well have been awarded a 7 or 9; in other words, 8 is the notional mid-point of a bracket of scale values (7, 8, 9), but a pupil's raw score

Table 5.3:   Score points and distributions of population for Stanines and Stens

| | | *Stanines* | | |
Unit SDs	Stanine	x̄ SD 100,15	Percentage in range	Cumulative percentage
	9		4.0	100
+1.75		126.25		
	8		6.6	96.4
+1.25		118.75		
	7		12.1	89.8
+0.75		111.25		
	6		17.5	77.7
+0.25		103.75		
	5		19.7	60.2
−0.25		96.25		
	4		17.5	40.5
−0.75		88.75		
	3		12.1	22.7
−1.25		81.25		
	2		6.6	10.6
−1.75		73.75		
	1		4.0	4.0

| | | *Stens* | | |
Unit SDs	Sten	x̄ SD 100,15	Percentage in range	Cumulative percentage
	10		2.3	100
+2.0		130		
	9		4.4	97.7
+1.5		122.5		
	8		9.2	93.3
+1.0		115		
	7		14.9	84.1
+0.5		107.5		
	6		19.2	69.2
0.0		100		
	5		19.2	50
−0.5		92.5		
	4		14.9	30.8
−1.0		85		
	3		9.2	15.9
−1.5		77.5		
	2		4.4	6.7
−1.0		70		
	1		2.3	2.3

might have placed him/her at one or other end of the range encompassed by the eighth Sten or Stanine.

Test authors who favour the use of Stanines because they provide a better form of report, which may be seen by parents and discussed with them, should remind users that the scale condenses a much wider range of scores into one represented by nine numerals. Furthermore, it could be said that each numeral is akin to a rank order, when the ranks are grouped into equal score bands; however, these bands contain different proportions of the population, with rather more than a half falling within the three middle bands of 4, 5 and 6.

Grades

The same argument about approximation underlies the use of broad grades or levels. One series of reasoning tests employs a five-grade classification which divides the population into successive bands of 10, 20, 40, 20 and 10 per cent, labelled grades A – E respectively. These divisions can be made on the basis of raw scores. However, it is worth noting that these arbitrary groupings are often justified as 'based on the normal curve'. The standardized normal score points ($\bar{x} = 100$, SD = 15) which divide these categories are E/D, 82.8; D/C, 92.2; C/B, 107.8; B/A, 119.2. Rounded to the nearest whole number these values are 81, 93, 108, 119.

The problem with this type of classification is that it is really too crude. For example, a pupil's raw score could occur near to the point equivalent to a standardized normal score of 93. If the pupil's score leads to a C-grade allocation, the user would have no indication that his/her performance was borderline with D grade; the best interpretation that can be given to C grade is 'about average', that is, near the middle of the middle 40 per cent. Clearly, in the instance cited this interpretation would be quite misleading. On occasions the distribution of grades quoted here is used for reporting test results to parents. Perhaps the best point in its favour is that only 30 per cent of the parents (of an 'average' group) have to be told that their son or daughter is 'below average'!

Other types of scale

Longitudinal
There is a growing tendency for tests developed in Britain to follow trends in the USA, where the investment of time, expertise and money is relatively larger, principally because pupils are tested more extensively throughout their school and college careers. Rather than promote single tests for specific applications, the publishers have produced series for successive age-groups. Within each series there are usually several sub-tests or separate tests, each scored in the same manner (usually by machine-read score sheets) and scaled in the same way.

Often the test questions are printed in a single booklet containing instructions to pupils about the level to be attempted and, in particular, the starting points for the various age-groups dealt with. The manuals for these tests may contain a scale which connects the results for the whole series. At its most basic this scale could comprise the overall raw score total for all of the tests accumulated age-group by age-group. For instance, if six age levels are each to attempt 40 items in a vocabulary sub-test, the sequence of items for the age-groups might be:

level	group		start		finish
A	1st-year Juniors	Items	1	to	40
B	2nd-year Juniors	Items	21	to	60
C	3rd-year Juniors	Items	41	to	80
D	4th-year Juniors	Items	61	to	100
E	1st-year Secondary	Items	81	to	120
F	2nd-year Secondary	Items	101	to	140

Here the overall raw score scale would be 140, but a third year Junior top-scorer could obtain only a maximum of 80; however, all children in this age band would be credited initially with 40 points.

This scheme would only be adopted when trials with adequate samples had shown that few pupils, if any, within an age-group obtained the extreme raw scores of 0, 1 or 2, or 38, 39 or 40. However, slow-learning pupils, or those whose progress is very advanced, could start at a lower or higher level, as appropriate. Results from these pupils would be included in the standardizations for the age-groups in the usual way.

There are numerous methods for creating longitudinal scales and as many labels for them, for example, the somewhat pretentious 'universal scale'. When the origin of a scale is age-group data, interpretation is via norm comparisons; when the basis is a curriculum, interpretation reflects the pupil's standard of performance or curriculum elements understood.

Item response

The overlapping test design, illustrated above, would be acceptable only if samples of pupils from the successive age-groups performed consistently at the sets of 20 items which make up the two halves of each test (except for levels A and F). For example, second-year Juniors would have items 40–60 in common with the third-year Juniors. Presumably these questions would be relatively hard for the second-year children and relatively easy for the third years. 'Easiness' or 'difficulty' would be apparent from the proportions of the trial samples giving correct answers. So for item 41 the second-year result might be 60 per cent correct, whilst for the third years this might be 80 per cent correct. Consider another item, say, number 60: if 15 per cent of the second-year sample give a correct answer, what percentage would we expect from the third years? To tabulate:

	item 41	item 60
2nd years	60%	15%
3rd years	80%	?

We can tackle this problem from several standpoints when certain assumptions are accepted. These are that the second- and third-year pupils are calling on the same attributes when interacting with the questions, and that the dimensions in the *implicit* variable which underlies the response levels are the same for both age-groups. From the data the ratio of second-year pupils responding correctly to items 41 and 60 is 4 : 1; also the second- to third-year ratio for item 41 is 3 : 4; hence the response level for third years to item 60 can be expected to be 20 per cent.

When the data from trials of test items fits into consistent patterns, of the kind illustrated, the hypotheses about dimensionality and attribute make-up are supported. The practical difficulties for the test constructor are the approximate values given by trial data and the need to test the assumptions stated above in a variety of contexts, for example, by comparing high-scoring group results with low-scoring groups of the same age, and by repeating the trials with fresh, independent samples of pupils. However, provided that the data is consistent and adequate, for substantial sets of questions scales can be built up or linked together through overlapping designs. In the case illustrated, if the 3 : 4 ratio between second and third years applied (approximately) to all 20 items in the common set, it would be expected that a pupil with a score of x in the second year would obtain a score of 4x/3 in the third year.

The same principle can be applied between sets of items regardless of age grouping, so that test scores on relatively 'easy' tests can be compared with scores on relatively difficult tests. Referring once more to the illustration, if for a given age-group ten items had the same facility (percentage correct) value as item 41 and ten the same facility value as item 60, a score on the 'hard' test of x would be expected to be equivalent to a score of 4x on the 'easy' test. Of course a pupil with a score of, say, 3 on the hard test would need at least 12 items at the easy test level before the *probability* of getting a question wrong might become manifest.

The main point of the illustration is to indicate that the relative difficulties of items (as shown by facility values) can be used to scale items on the basis of the response probabilities, provided that these relativities are consistent for samples representative of pupils. Also large numbers of items can be scaled by linking one trial set with others using overlapping designs. A result is that banks or pools of items can be established, each item with a scale value which indicates the estimated relative difficulty when compared with the other items in the bank. The relative difficulty scale, in theory, is infinitely extensive, but it can include items which are appropriate for the extremes of pupil performance both within and across age ranges. Accordingly tests can be chosen from a bank to suit particular purposes; also the distribution of item relative difficulties and overall level can be matched to a testing purpose. In practice, the scales developed from item-response data usually involve a transformation with natural logarithms and numerical constants; these produce scales labelled 'wits' or 'logits'. These are ratio scales: there is no natural zero point, but the divisions are ratio units and so are said to be interpretable in additive and multiplicative terms. Hence a pupil tested for a second time whose score on such a scale is doubled is regarded as having twice the amount of the attribute when first assessed.

It should be noted that not all attributes, or measures of them, produce the consistency of item-response patterns which is required as a condition of applying the theory, and that there has been considerable controversy about applying the methods for certain purposes such as longitudinal surveys. However, where the consistencies have been established through properly conducted trials, the results are as acceptable as any other method of scaling test performance. The most notable example of a test with this type of scale used extensively to cope with the wide variation of performances within and between age-groups is the *British Ability Scales*. Their use is restricted to psychologists or teachers who have been specifically trained in administration and interpretation. There might well be occasions, however, when such a specialist should confer with teachers and refer to the test results. In this event it would be essential for both parties to refer to the appropriate manual to establish common understanding of the scales and the norm tables.

CHAPTER 6
Handling Test Data

The preceding chapters have introduced a number of statistical concepts; some are fundamental, such as 'population', 'sample' and 'variable', others are instrumental such as the types of scale. This chapter has the aim of encouraging teachers to use test data descriptively and to examine its various implications.

Several related notions are involved but these all stem from the idea that a distribution of a variable can be expressed as an average figure, the arithmetic mean, with each separate score deviating from it by a particular amount. As we have seen, classes or other groupings of pupils are samples from a population and test results are the product of a one-off occasion affected by a range of factors. These affect individuals in the sample and also influence the group average performance, expressed as the mean.

To illustrate this point imagine that several children were asked to measure a length of cloth which was wrinkled and creased from being kept in a cupboard. Some would standardize the conditions by ironing the cloth, others would try stretching it out; some would use the tape carefully, others would make mistakes in reading the scale. It might not be possible to measure an exact length, but it is highly likely that the best estimate of a 'true' length would be the average of those made by the children. Under these circumstances the errors made by individuals are assumed to have been evened out by averaging. This illustration shows that estimates of the likely amount of individual error, and their effects on the group mean, should be examined when results are interpreted.

The term that is used to indicate the probable spread of estimates of error is 'standard error'. In some respects, this is somewhat misleading as it refers to the estimated standard deviation of certain measures. For individual scores this SD is called the Standard Error of Score; for group means it is called the Standard Error of the Mean. As will be shown, both call on the normal curve model to define conventional limits which assist with deciding whether or not the inherent variability in the results obtained makes decision-taking defensible.

In the latter part of the chapter the focus is on the association between pairs of variables. Often pairs of measures obtained for each pupil in a group can be examined for educational implications. For example, mathematics and reading test results from several classes of children were examined to see in what ways reading attainment was associated with mathematics attainment. It was found that pupils who were below the mean in Reading did progressively less well at Mathematics; for those above the mean for Reading the relationship with Mathematics was negligible. One method for estimating the extent of any relationship is to calculate a 'correlation coefficient', this again is a kind of average showing how well the pairs of results from each pupil are matched. Another method is to classify each individual according to test performance and then to see whether different categories of pupils have certain characteristics.

The techniques outlined in the chapter can be used confidently by teachers, as I have seen on many occasions. But all too frequently pupils are tested and their results listed with no follow-up analysis done. Computer-based test-scoring systems usually provide some of the information such as the standard errors for individual scores on separate tests and the standard errors for group means. Computer programs too are available for other kinds of data analyses, as described later. These require orderly data presentation in formats suited to the programs.

Why data analyses are important can be illustrated by an example which concerns tests in a first school given by the head as part of the LEA 'screening' procedure. The head customarily administered the two tests supplied by the authority and marked the scripts. The teachers were then told who the low-scoring children were – usually there were no surprises. However, the teachers were quite depressed to find how far down the scale the slower children came and were not encouraged by the head's remarks about the children who were 'falling behind'. One year the class lists of results were given to the teachers and the means were calculated for one class. It was found that for the Mathematics test the mean was about 108, and for Reading the mean was about 106. As these results were somewhat higher than the means for the LEA, the teacher's view of the class (and the tests) was transformed. These results are discussed statistically in the section on evaluating mean scores.

For readers who hitherto have tested pupils and then considered only the scores for individuals, some practical work is proposed. This is based on the results from two tests given to two groups of children. For the work you need (1) two lists of children's names, their ages in years and completed months when tested, with raw scores from two tests, all arranged in columns, and (2) an electronic calculator with square root or with statistical functions for mean, standard deviation and correlation, or a computer with a program for the same statistics. In this chapter the groups are referred to as Class A and Class B and the tests as Test 1 and Test 2. The data for at least one test should be obtained from a standardized norm-referenced test; the other set of test data could be results from a school examination, a class test or another standardized test or 'levels' from national curriculum tests. Though formulas and examples are given, the emphasis throughout the chapter is on principles relating to the interpretation of test information.

Graphic representation

Test data for groups is more readily appreciated when its distribution is shown graphically. The procedure is basically straightforward as it consists of counting the frequency with which a given score occurs among the sample of pupils. It is usually preferable to group scores into class intervals. One method is to peruse the list of scores to find the two extreme results – this gives the range. Say that the 30 pupils in Class A on Test 1 had obtained a range of 33 points, from 21 to 54; this number of pupils and the range suggests a class interval of 5 points. A tally arranged in class intervals might look like this:

21 – 25 26 – 30 31 – 35 36 – 40 41 – 45 46 – 50 51 – 55
  ///   //   ////   ЦИТ //   ЦИТ /   ЦИТ   ///
   3   2   4   7   6   5   3

This data could be portrayed as a histogram or as a frequency polygon, as shown in Figure 6.1.

Figure 6.1:   **Examples of frequency distribution shown by histogram and frequency polygon**

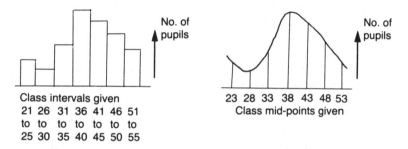

The histogram base in the figure is set out in fives, whereas the frequency polygon base is set out to show the mid-point of each class interval. Most statistics computer programs produce graphs which are histograms built up with asterisks. For class teachers there is some advantage in drawing the graphs by hand as this procedure brings home the position achieved by each pupil among the group. The graph shows the *frequency distribution* for a sample of pupils on a given variable. For the national testing levels, instead of class intervals the baseline will show each level administered either for each component or aggregates for each subject.

Exercise: Readers with lists of test scores should decide on a suitable class interval for one of the tests when both classes, A and B, are considered together. This can be done by dividing the score range into about ten divisions. After tallying the frequencies, draw the histogram of the frequency distribution.

Mean, Standard Deviation and Standard Error of the Mean

The calculation of the mean and SD for a distribution of scores has been described in Chapter 5. These statistics form the basis for a yardstick, that is, the Standard Error of the Mean, which is helpful when the results for a group or groups of pupils are evaluated.

In the case of the screening test results, referred to earlier, it was found that the Mathematics and Reading test class means were about 8 and 6 points respectively above the standardization population mean of 100. This information gave the teacher a different view of the class, especially when it was pointed out that the LEA means, for an LEA population of 7000 or so pupils, were also higher than the standardized mean by almost 5 points, for both tests.

In fact the class concerned happened to be quite close to the LEA means. But even had the means been quite a few points different, there would probably have been grounds for accepting that the results were merely part of the general run of events, in which case there would be no cause for the teacher to be worried. The reason is that sub-samples within a population can vary quite markedly.

Consider that the standardization sample raw score result and the LEA raw score result gave rise to standardized mean scores of 100 and about 105 respectively. The five-point difference would be significant because both results came from large numbers. But each of these groups would be made up of many classes of pupils from a large number of schools, each class being a sub-sample. These separate sub-samples would each produce a mean, so there is a distribution of means created in both the national standardization exercise and the LEA survey. The distribution of *means* from samples tend to pile up around the general population mean; indeed the distribution of means tends to be normal in shape (and degree of dispersion is indicated by a standard deviation value).

To distinguish the dispersion of sample means (for a given
size of sample) from the dispersion that applies to a set of
individual scores (the SD) the term Standard Error of the Mean
is used (written as SE_m). In the case of the LEA, the SE_m can
be found by computing the obtained SD divided by the square
root of the number of pupils. For instance, with SD of 13, say,

$$SE_m = \frac{SD}{\sqrt{N}} = \frac{13}{\sqrt{7000}} = \frac{13}{83.67} = 0.155.$$

(Compared with the population SD of 13, the value of 0.155
is relatively small.)

The SE_m of a sub-sample mean can be estimated from a
similar formula, that is, the SD divided by the square root of
the number of pupils minus one. Say the SD for one teacher's
class of 35 pupils was 8.5, the SE of the class mean would be
estimated from:

$$SE_m = \frac{8.5}{\sqrt{34}} = \frac{8.5}{5.83} = 1.46$$

(a relatively large value). This latter value shows that the SD
for the distribution of means for samples of this size is estimated to be 1.46. One SD on both sides of the mean
encompasses a range of ±1.46, that is, 2.92 points. The scale
value of the SE_m range is applied to produce a *confidence
interval*, as explained below.

To recapitulate, different proportions of a sample of normally distributed values are related to corresponding areas
under the normal curve (Figure 6.2). So plus and minus $1SE_m$,
for a distribution of means, encompasses 68 per cent of cases,
that is, there is a 68 per cent probability that a sample of size
N would have a mean in this confidence interval. A larger
interval or band can be obtained by accepting a higher probability; for example, plus and minus $2SE_m$ would give a 96 per
cent level of probability (meaning that for samples of size N
there is a 96 per cent probability that the mean for any sample
will fall within the confidence interval given by $±2SE_m$). Con-
ventionally two scale bands indicating the magnitude of confidence limits are distinguished, one at 95 and the other at 99

Figure 6.2: Areas under the normal curve by deviation units

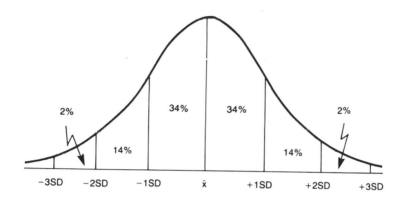

per cent. The former has an interval of 1.96 standard error values, whilst the latter has an interval of 2.58 standard error values. These confidence limits are often referred to, alternatively, as the 5 and 1 per cent levels of significance.

The meaning of these two levels of significance is stated in terms of probabilities. For the narrower confidence interval there is a one in 20 chance that the sample mean obtained is not a member of the population of means for randomly drawn samples of the same size. For the wider confidence band the probability that the sample mean is not a member of the same population is one in 100. Put the other way round, the odds respectively are 19 to 1 and 99 to 1 that when a mean value lies within a confidence band there is no significant difference between the sample and the parent population.

Hence to compare a teacher's class mean for Reading scores of 106 with the LEA population mean of 105 entails finding the difference between the means (in this case 1 point) and comparing this with the standard error applied to a confidence interval. With $SE_m = 1.46$, there is no need to consider the 5 and 1 per cent levels because the difference of one point is obviously smaller than the standard error.

However, suppose the class mean had been as low as 102 points. The difference from the LEA mean of 105 is three points. The two significance levels give rise to confidence bands of $1.46 \times 1.96 = 2.86$ at 5 per cent, and $1.46 \times 2.58 = 3.77$ at 1 per cent. Clearly, only one of these values is less than the difference between the means of three points, so this difference can be regarded as statistically significant beyond the 5 per cent level of significance, but not up to the 1 per cent level. Expressed another way, we could say that there is somewhat higher than one chance in 20 that this class difference of three points below the county mean arose from chance effects.

Compared with the standardization (population) mean of 100, a sub-sample mean which differs by more than the 2.86 points of the 95 per cent confidence band could be regarded as interesting. So we might decide to set upper and lower limits of 100 ± 2.86 and *only* look at classes whose means fall above 102.86 or below 97.14.

The principle which operates when groups are being compared is quite simple, as the example illustrates. It is that larger samples (from a population) produce more certainty with regard to estimating the population mean. The formula used earlier on has square root of the sample size minus one in the denominator; the standard error is thus reduced approximately in proportion to the square of the sample numbers. Thus to halve the standard error of the mean obtained from a sample of size N by enlarging the sample entails quadrupling the sample size. For a sample of 101 pupils $\sqrt{(N-1)} = 10$, so that the SE_m is 10 per cent of the SD for the sample. For a sample of 401 pupils, $\sqrt{(N-1)} = 20$; for a sample of 1601 pupils, $\sqrt{(N-1)} = 40$. Towards the other extreme, for 26 pupils, $\sqrt{(N-1)} = 5$.

The implications of this arithmetic are that comparisons between small samples and very large LEA population or standardization sample means are unlikely to show significant differences at even the lower level of significance (5 per cent) *unless* the sample SD is also relatively very small. This situation can occur when there is a concentration of pupils' score at or near the same standard (and therefore little deviation from the sample mean). Much of this is commonsense.

In the case of the class teacher whose attention was directed to the lower-attaining pupils, calculation of the group means (as if the pupils were a random sample) was extremely reassuring. And even if the means for their classes had been significantly different at one or other level of significance, there would have been strong educational inferences to be drawn. For example, had the difference between the LEA mean and the class mean been relatively large, the class might have been regarded as exceptional. A significantly lower than LEA mean (beyond the 1 per cent level) could have implied that additional support for the teacher and children should be considered. A significantly higher than LEA mean might have implied that the reading curriculum aims and content should be reviewed and, possibly, less time given to it.

Relevant formulae for Class A, Test 1, are:

Mean, $\bar{x}_1 = \dfrac{\Sigma x_1}{N_A}$ Sum of pupils' scores divided by number in class

$SD_1 = \sqrt{\dfrac{\Sigma(x_1 - \bar{x}_1)^2}{N_A}}$ Square root of the means of the totalled squared deviations

An alternative formula for calculating the SD utilizes pupils' total scores directly; there is no need to find each pupil's deviation $(x - \bar{x})$ from the mean. The formula is:

$SD_1 = \sqrt{\left(\dfrac{\Sigma x_1^2 - \bar{x}_1^2}{N_A}\right)}$ Square root of the mean of squared scores minus the mean squared

$SE_{m1} = \dfrac{SD_1}{\sqrt{(N_A - 1)}}$ Standard deviation divided by number in group minus one

Worked example: For convenience, to keep the size of the numbers lower and the arithmetic simpler, a constant of 80 has been deducted from pupils' scores, as shown in the second column of the following table.

serial numbers	pupils' names	test scores (x)	score minus 80 (x − 80)	square of (x − 80)
1	Bell	84	4	16
2	Briggs	92	12	144
3	Cass	130	50	2500
4	Churns	116	36	1296
5	. . .	112	32	1024
6	. . .	101	21	441
7	. . .	97	17	289
8	. . .	112	32	1024
9	. . .	104	24	576
10	. . .	93	13	169
11	. . .	99	19	361
12	. . .	104	24	576
13	. . .	105	25	625
14	. . .	98	18	324
15	. . .	92	12	144
16	. . .	97	17	289
17	. . .	117	37	1369
18	. . .	91	11	121
19	Sands	103	23	529
20	Sharma	96	16	256
21	Smith	105	25	625
22	Tandy	140	60	3600
23	West	87	7	49
			$\Sigma x = $ 535	$\Sigma x^2 = $ 16,347 Totals

Mean class score minus 80 is:

$$\frac{\Sigma(x - 80)}{N} = \frac{535}{23} = 23.26$$

Mean = 23.26 + 80 = 103.26

Standard Deviation using mean for score minus 80 value is:

$$\sqrt{\left(\frac{16,347}{23} - 23.26^2\right)}$$

$$= \sqrt{(710.74 - 541.02)}$$

$$= \sqrt{169.72}$$

$$SD = 13.02$$

(The spread of scores as indicated by the SD is not affected by deducting the constant of 80 from each score.)

Standard Error of Mean is:

$$\frac{13.02}{\sqrt{22}}$$

$$-\frac{13.02}{4.69}$$

$$= 2.78$$

For the 5 per cent level of significance limits are $SE_m \times 1.96$. For this example $2.78 \times 1.96 = 5.44$, hence the confidence band on either side of the mean is ±5.44.

Interpretation: The class mean of 103.26 differs from the standardization (population) mean of 100 by 3.26 points. As this value is within the 5 per cent level confidence band, the difference is not significant at the 5 per cent level. Accordingly, the class can be regarded as at or near the average for the population. For the class to have been regarded as clearly above average the mean should have been higher than 105.44.

Note: There is a distinction between educational significance and statistical significance. The latter is useful for deciding whether to take a result seriously in cases where it is not fairly obvious from the data. In the example given above a class mean of 115, say, would have made a statistical significance test superfluous.

Exercise: Those readers who have class lists of scores should use a calculator or a computer to find the means. SD and SE_m

for classes A and B for the standardized test score. The SE_m values should then be multiplied by the constant of 1.96 to give the 5 per cent confidence interval for each variable. Assuming that the population mean is the one given in the relevant test manual (usually 100), decide whether each class difference from the standardized mean is significantly different at the 5 per cent level of confidence.

Interpreting individual scores

The idea that a test score is an estimate of a pupil's position on a scale which represents a variable has been stressed in previous chapters. How good an estimate is depends on certain qualities inherent in each test. These qualities relate to how well the measure represents the attribute under consideration and also whether the measure obtained is unbiased or the product of an erratic instrument. This section deals with the measure as an accurate and reliable instrument of assessment.

The two concepts can be separated, as a mundane illustration shows: a vintage car petrol gauge shows 'full' when the tank is topped up to overflowing and 'empty' when about half the fuel has been used. The gauge is not accurate, but it is reliable; in other words, it is systematically biased but consistent in different places and on different days, the measure is repeatable. Despite its lack of precision, the car owner finds the estimate given by the gauge useful because he can reliably estimate the 'true' measure of petrol in the tank after taking distance travelled into account.

In testing, three conceptions of reliability have been developed. One is internal consistency (the extent to which the test items each contribute towards the total score); the second is equivalence (the extent to which different tests of the same attribute produce comparable scores); and the third is stability (the extent to which total scores are replicated if pupils are tested on two separate occasions).

If a test is not internally consistent, the implication is that some of the items can be answered by drawing on other attributes than the one which is the object of the test. In this case, the test lacks homogeneity. In fact it is the inconsistency between individuals who take the test which gives rise to its unreliability. For instance, if two people both scored 50 on a 100-item test of historical events, but both answered different questions correctly, their *results* could hardly be regarded as comparable. If many other pupils obtained scores in a similar way, the test *as a whole* would be regarded as producing internally inconsistent results.

Equivalence between two tests of the same attribute would be demonstrated if a list of pupils' scores on both tests corre lated highly. This would show most readily in the rank orders, that is, the first pupil on one test would either be first or high up the list, and so on down to the lowest-ranked pupil. Correlation is shown by the symbol r, and between two variables A and B, the symbol format is r_{AB}. When the two score lists for a set of pupils correspond exactly (that is, the pairs of ranks are matched all the way through the list), r has a maximum value of 1.0. If the ranks are inversely related (that is, the top pupil on one test is bottom on the other, the middle pupil is middle on both, etc.) the value of r is −1.0. Higgledy-piggledy rank pairs produce a value for r of 0. In fact correlations can be computed from the test scores without the need to produce rank orders.

Also two tests can be made 'parallel' to the extent of having the same content areas, structure and number of items; additionally, the items can be interchangeable between tests. Such a deliberate attempt to create equivalence might be expected to yield values of r which approach the maximum of 1.0. In fact values of around 0.9 are more usual, partly because the two tests have to be taken by the same pupils on different occasions (performance varies over a timespan).

This difficulty also besets the estimation of stability in test results, known as 'test re-test reliability'. If children are given the test for a second time immediately after the first administration, they are likely to recall some of their responses and benefit from practice. But if the re-test is delayed considerably, their performance might well improve because of genuine learning, though some may progress more than others. In practice, stability coefficients are obtained from test administrations between one to six weeks apart. In these cases coefficients of r can exceed 0.9.

Of course, if scoring involves judges in interpreting mark keys or other assessment criteria, as in written school examinations, there is likely to be less equivalence between test versions or consistency between the parts of a test or stability over time. This means that an individual pupil's score might fluctuate because of differences between judges (when more than one marks a set of scripts) or inconsistency on the part of single judges. When groups of assessors meet to discuss their application of mark schemes or criteria in so called moderation meetings, they are attempting to make their judgements more equivalent (see Postscript, p. 215, for an outline of the procedures). An aspect which is seldom addressed explicitly, though it should be, is the equivalence of standards over time when *different* tasks or test papers are given to successive populations of pupils year after year, as in National Curriculum assessments or external examinations. (Sub-samples could be given samples of tasks given in previous years to estimate the variation due to tasks; but this would require more time, money and planning.)

Commonsense says that when a test result arises from an unreliable test, the score is only an approximation of that which would have been obtained had a perfectly reliable test been used. The question, then, is what range of score is it reasonable to take as the band within which the 'true' score would have occurred. There are many ways of estimating the size of this band, though the choice of the reliability coefficient used in the calculation can have a substantial effect. Once again, the concept of a sample of results normally distributed is useful. The reason is that the standard deviation of such a hypothetical distribution of test scores is taken to give an index called the Standard Error of Score.

Relevant formula:

$$SE_{score} = SD \sqrt{(1 - r_{AB})}$$ Standard deviation from a population or sample multiplied by the square root of one minus the reliability coefficient.

In this formula r_{AB} is the estimated reliability coefficient obtained from correlating two parallel forms of a test, A and B (other types of reliability coefficient are used, but it is not necessary to cite these formulae here).

Worked example: Given the following data:
  Test standardization SD = 15
  Test re-test reliability = 0.84

$$SE_{score} = \sqrt{(1 - 0.84)}$$
$$= 15 \sqrt{0.16}$$
$$= 15 \times 0.4 = 6.0 \text{ points.}$$

Interpretation: This standard error implies that we can be confident, with odds of 68 to 32, that a pupil's 'true' score would fall within a band of plus and minus one standard errors, that is, 12 points. This band is applied to the score obtained by anyone taking the test. Thus a pupil who obtained, say 92, would have a confidence band of plus and minus one standard error between 86 and 98. As would be expected, a wider band gives even more confidence that the range captures the 'true' score. Thus at the 95 per cent confidence limits the band would be $1.96 \times 6 = 11.76$ points on either side of an obtained score, and for the 1 per cent limits the range would be twice $2.58 \times 6 = 2 \times 15.48 = 30.96$. This figure implies that a pupil who obtained a score in excess of 115 is hardly likely to be average (have a 'true' score at the mean) as the odds are about 99 to 1 against.

The main point of the foregoing discussion is to underline the approximate nature of the score obtained by a pupil and, correspondingly, to emphasize the importance of using tests which have been made as reliable as possible by the test authors. Test manuals ought to give appropriate reliability data (sample sizes, school and demographic details) and the type(s) of any coefficient(s) calculated. Furthermore, the user should find clear statements of the standard error of score and, ideally, illustrations showing the range of scores associated with certain confidence levels. There are many procedures and formulae for estimating test reliability, which differ according to type, that is, internal consistency, equival-

Figure 6.3:   **Example of recording a pupil's score on a standardized scale within a confidence band**

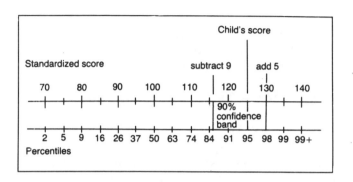

ence or stability. Figure 6.3 illustrates how a pupil's scores can be recorded to show the confidence band.

Hopefully the preceding discussion shows that treating test scores as precise measures is not sound practice. Thus comments, for instance, that a child scoring 99 on a standardized reading test, as compared with a previous (and different test) score of 104, has fallen below average can be seen to be nonsensical. A five-point difference would be something like the standard error of score associated with results for both tests. By thinking along the lines that the separate results are each a sample taken from a distribution with an SD of about five it can be appreciated that the results might well have overlapped.

Exercises: (a) Ascertain for the standardized test, Test 1 or Test 2 (or both), the reliability coefficients cited in the manual(s) and the standard error of score(s), if given. If not given, calculate the confidence intervals for 1SE and for the 5 per cent level of significance (that is, 1SE × 1.96); round the results *up* to the nearest whole number. (b) Run down the Test 1 and Test 2 lists of scores for one class and asterisk any pupil whose scores are further apart than the average of the test standard errors of score. If you can determine only one standard error, from test manual information, estimate the other as one-fifth of the SD of the scores obtained by the class.

Comparing two groups of pupils

When two separate groups of pupils take the same test, it is possible to compare the mean scores for each group by treating them as random samples from the same population. Had this been the case, it might be anticipated that the means would be similar. Of course a few large differences might occur because of chance (for example, guessing multiple-choice answers, more children disliking the test situation in one group, and so on).

The procedure with two groups to compare is, first, to calculate the respective group means, SD and SE_m, then to apply the formula for standard error of the difference between means. The result is an estimate of the standard deviation of a distribution of differences between means for samples of the sizes achieved. Using the normal curve model once again, the confidence intervals for evaluating differences of certain magnitude can be found by forming what is termed a 'critical ratio' (CR).

Relevant formula:

$$SEdiff_{1,2} = \sqrt{[(SE_{m1})^2 + (SE_{m2})^2]}$$

The standard error of the difference between means is the square root of the sum of the squared standard error of the means for both groups

$$\text{Critical ratio, CR} = \frac{Diff_{1,2}}{SEdiff_{1,2}}$$

Difference between the group means, divided by the standard error of the difference

Worked example: Evaluate the difference between two successive year-groups of pupils, groups 1 and 2, who obtain standardized mean scores of 98 and 102. There are 122 and 145 pupils respectively in the groups; the SDs are 10 and 14.

First, find the standard error of the means for both groups:

$$SE_{m1} = \frac{10}{\sqrt{(122 - 1)}} = \frac{10}{\sqrt{121}} = \frac{10}{11} = 0.91$$

$$SE_{m2} = \frac{14}{\sqrt{(145 - 1)}} = \frac{14}{\sqrt{144}} = \frac{14}{12} = 1.17$$

In the formula $SEdiff_{1,2} = \sqrt{(0.91^2 + 1.17^2)}$
$$= \sqrt{2.19}$$
$$= 1.48$$

Then form a critical ratio:

$$CR = \frac{102 - 98}{1.48} = \frac{4}{1.48} = 2.70$$

Interpretation: Hypothetically two groups chosen at random from a population would have the same mean, that is, the difference between means would be zero. But a difference can be anticipated due to chance factors. With a value of 2.70, the CR exceeds the significance level for 99 per cent of cases, that is, a value of 2.58; in this case we can regard the difference of four points as showing a highly significant difference between the groups.

The t-ratio: When the two groups to be compared are small (less than 30 is the usual limit), it is necessary to use an adjusted critical ratio set of values, known as the t-distribution. Computer programs for evaluating differences between means usually have the t-distributions incorporated, but it is as well to check, otherwise any small group comparisons could be misleading. The formula for calculating the value of t for two samples which differ in size is:

$$t = \cfrac{M_1 - M_2}{\sqrt{\left[\cfrac{\Sigma(x_1 - \bar{x}_1)^2 + \Sigma(x_2 - \bar{x}_2)^2}{N_1 + N_2 - 2} \; \cfrac{N_1 + N_2}{N_1 N_2} \right]}}$$

The reader will recognize the terms in the first bracket of the denominator, $\Sigma(x_1 - \bar{x}_1)^2$ and $\Sigma(x_2 - x_2)^2$, as the sums of the squared deviations for the respective variables; these are usually referred to more briefly as 'the sums of the squares'.

In this case t is the critical ratio, and this is evaluated according to the 'degrees of freedom' which samples of the size N_1 and N_2 have to vary; that is, $N_1 + N_2 - 2$ (the combined samples minus two). The idea in determining degrees of freedom is that with any pupil in a distribution taken as the reference-point, there are $N - 1$ variations from it which are possible.

Re-working the example used above, but with class sizes of 30 and 24 and test score SDs of 8 and 6.5 (smaller groups usually have relatively smaller score dispersions), illustrates how the difference between means of 98 and 102 should be interpreted. First, we need to find the 'sum of squares' for both groups, to give values for the $(x - \bar{x})^2$ terms. From the SD formula

$$\sqrt{\left[\frac{\Sigma(x - \bar{x})^2}{N} \right]} \qquad \text{for the first class of 30 pupils}$$

substitution gives:

$$8 = \sqrt{\left[\frac{\Sigma(x - \bar{x}_1)^2}{30} \right]}$$

squaring both sides gives:

$$64 = \frac{\Sigma(x_1 - \bar{x}_1)^2}{30}$$

hence $30 \times 64 = \Sigma(x - \bar{x}_1)^2$

so $\Sigma(x_1 - \bar{x}_1)^2 = 1920$ (the sum of squared difference of each pupil's score from the class mean).

Similarly, for the second class:

$$6.5 = \sqrt{\left[\frac{\Sigma(x_2 - \bar{x}_2)^2}{24}\right]}$$

squaring both sides gives:

$$42.25 = \frac{\Sigma(x_2 - \bar{x}_2)^2}{24}$$

hence $24 \times 42.25 = \Sigma(x_2 - \bar{x}_2)^2$

so $\Sigma(x_2 - \bar{x}_2)^2 = 1020$.

Using these values, class sizes and means to find t:

$$t = \frac{102 - 98}{\sqrt{\left(\frac{1920 + 1020}{30 + 24 - 2} \times \frac{30 + 24}{30 \times 24}\right)}}$$

$$= \frac{4}{\sqrt{\left(\frac{2940}{52} \times \frac{54}{720}\right)}}$$

$$= \frac{4}{\sqrt{(56.54 \times 0.075)}} = \frac{4}{\sqrt{4.24}} = \frac{4}{2.06} = 1.94$$

As t has a value slightly lower than 2.01, the 5 per cent confidence value of t for 50 degrees of freedom (the nearest to 52) given in the statistical table, the difference of four points may be regarded as attributable to chance variation. In other words, the four-point difference is not significant at the 5 per cent level of confidence.

We can see from this example that group size is a critical factor when group means are compared (as reference back to the discussion on sample size on p. 105 confirms).

Difference between means for correlated scores: A different case has to be considered when the same group of pupils is compared for their performance on two variables. The reason is that there is likely to be a degree of correlation, and this affects the conclusions to be drawn from a difference between the means for the two measures. Accordingly, it is necessary to calculate the correlation between the variables. *Relevant formula* (when the variables are designated as A and B):

$$SE_{diff.AB\ corr} = \sqrt{\left[(SE_{mA})^2 + (SE_{mB})^2 - 2r.SE_{mA}.SE_{mB}\right]}$$

that is, the square root of the sum of the standard errors of the means for both tests A and B, minus twice the product of the correlation coefficient and the standard errors, when r is the correlation coefficient.

Worked example: Imagining that a class with 26 pupils given two tests, A and B, produces data as follows:

Test A Mean 93   Test B Mean 99
SD   7   SD 5.6
Correlation, r_{AB} = 0.68

First, the separate standard errors are found:

$$SE_{mA} = \frac{7}{\sqrt{(26-1)}} = \frac{7}{5} = 1.4$$

$$SE_{mB} = \frac{5.6}{\sqrt{(26-1)}} = \frac{5.6}{5} = 1.12$$

In the formula:

$$SE_{diff.AB} = \sqrt{[(1.4)^2 + (1.12)^2 - 2 \times 0.68 \times 1.4 \times 1.12]}$$

$$= \sqrt{(1.96 + 1.25 - 2.13)}$$

$$= \sqrt{(3.21 - 2.13)}$$

$$= \sqrt{1.08}$$

$$= 1.04$$

The critical ratio is found by dividing the difference between the test means by the relevant standard error. The difference is $99 - 93 = 6$ points:

$$CR = \frac{6}{1.04} = 5.77$$

Interpretation: As this value exceeds 2.787, the value for t at the 1 per cent level of confidence for 25 degrees of freedom, the difference between the results can be accepted as highly significant. Thus, if these were scores from two standardized Mathematics Tests taken in successive terms, it would be reasonable to think that the class as a whole had improved to a higher general standard.

Exercises: (a) Using an electronic calculator or a computer, for either Class A or Class B, calculate the means for the two test results; also calculate the SD, the SE_m and the correlation coefficient (see Figure 6.5 and associated text). With this data, work out the critical ratio and evaluate the difference between mA and mB. (*Reminder:* if CR is below 1.96, significance does not reach the 5 per cent level; if CR is above 2.58, the 1 per cent level is exceeded.) Should the class have 25 or fewer members, it will be necessary to find statistical tables for values of t appropriate to the degrees of freedom, that is, number in class minus one $(N - 1)$. (b) Carry out a similar exercise to compare the means for Class A and Class B on either Test 1 or Test 2.

Comparing two scores for an individual

This aspect of handling test scores is extremely important. Regrettably the technical points which need close attention are more frequently ignored than taken into account. Their importance stems from the fact that differences between test scores are relatively more prone to error than either of the parent scores.

Reference back to the section on the SE score for a single test shows that the variability associated with any obtained score is dependent on two factors, that is, the test reliability coefficient and the standard deviation of a score distribution (obtained from a sample of pupils). Clearly, test score differences must take both test reliabilities into account as well as the correlation between pupils' scores. One formula for estimating the reliability of the difference between two scores, x_A and x_B, is:

$$r_{\text{diff.AB}} = \frac{r_A + r_B - 2r_{AB}}{2(1 - r_{AB})}$$

when r_{AB} is the inter-test correlation coefficient, with r_A and r_B as the test reliability coefficients.

To illustrate how the factors operate, suppose that the data is as follows: $r_A = 0.9$, $r_B = 0.8$, $r_{AB} = 0.6$. With these quite high reliabilities, and with the tests moderately correlated, the formula gives:

$$r_{\text{diff.AB}} = \frac{0.9 + 0.8 - 2 \times 0.6}{2(1 - 0.6)}$$

$$= \frac{1.7 - 1.2}{2 - 1.2} = \frac{0.5}{0.8} = 0.625 \text{ (only a middling value)}$$

The difference reliability coefficient could be used in the formula for an individual score standard error to give the standard error of the difference; but it is really necessary only to understand that score differences tend to be less reliable than the respective parent variables. Another point is that high correlation between two variables gives rise to less reliable differences. Hence any differences which occur are mainly error variations. Consequently, it is necessary to examine correlations between tests for the sample of pupils concerned. However, if only a few pupils are being considered, data from comparable samples will be necessary, otherwise sensible estimates of inter-correlations will suffice.

As an approximate guide, if two tests have an average reliability of 0.90 and are correlated at a low level, about 0.30, the difference between scores for interpretation at the 5 per cent level of significance is about the combined standard errors of score. If the average reliability for the tests was around 0.80

and the inter-correlation was about 0.5, the difference at the same level of confidence would be about 1½ times the combined standard errors.

Usually tests of the same attribute correlate quite highly. So if a pupil is compared on, say, two tests of English given a year apart, relatively small score differences would be regarded as chance variations. Larger differences, say from ½ to 1 of the averaged test standard errors, could be regarded as a trend to be noted. Beyond this level larger differences could be interpreted as a marked educational gain or loss.

Profiles

Test manuals for batteries of tests ought to give trial data which allows the user to see how differences between pairs of test results can be evaluated. One fairly simple way is to provide a set of graphic scales and to specify score sheets which lead the user to mark each pupil's result as a confidence band. An example is given in Figure 6.4. Here the bands would represent the standard error of score (that is, one standard deviation in estimated distribution of 'true' score relative to an obtained score). Where the confidence bands overlap, the score differences would be regarded as probably due to chance. Where there is no overlap, differences would be regarded as significant. In this example the A vs B difference would be ignored whilst the C vs A and C vs B differences would be interpreted.

When several tests are incorporated in a battery, it is common practice to join score points on a results chart and call the outcome a profile. This procedure tends to overlook the comparison of confidence bands, and it also imposes an order on the results which encourages the examination of adjacent pairs of results rather than all possible pairs. For example, a battery of six tests gives rise to $5 + 4 + 3 + 2 + 1$ pairs of results, that is, 15 in all. To illustrate this point, consider a profile for three ability tests and three attainment tests, all scaled to normalized standard scores with a mean of 100 and SD of 15 (Figure 6.5). The test scores shown are at the mid-point of the confidence bands of ±1SE score.

Figure 6.4: Illustration of profile scores with confidence bands of one standard error of score

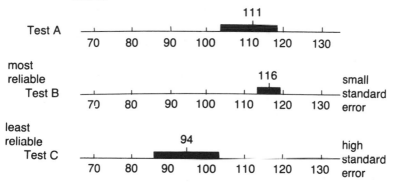

The presentation in the figure encourages 'at a glance' interpretation along the lines that Pupil X is an under-achiever and Pupil Y is somewhat below average in ability and of average attainment (is this an over-achiever!). When interpretation along these lines occurs, there is severe reduction of the meaning available in the data. This happens because (1) the order of variables in the list is somewhat arbitrary, (2) the zig-zag of five lines acquires undue importance and (3) the obtained scores are emphasized, even though the score confidence bands are drawn on the chart.

Profiles can be useful: the uniform presentation of results offers a framework for interpretation. But all of the data should be examined critically, keeping in mind the technical question: 'how reliable are the differences which are being compared?'

Exercise: Find the correlation (see Figure 6.5 and associated text) between Test 1 and Test 2 for Classes A and B combined as a single group. Then use this coefficient in the formula given above to estimate the reliability of the difference between the pairs of scores for the individuals in your sample. The reliability coefficients you use can be those given in the test manuals; if only one reliability coefficient is available from a manual, use a value of 0.85 for the other test.

Figure 6.5: Two graphic profiles compared

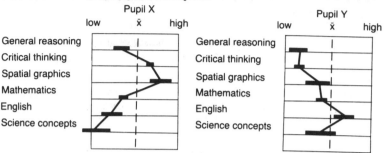

Following up test results: predicting from test data

Most of the ways of handling test data described so far have
entailed the use of descriptive statistics such as raw score
range, mean, SD, etc. However, when the probable significance
of the descriptive data was examined, by reference to confidence levels, the information was being examined to see
whether certain inferences might be defensible. It has been
argued elsewhere that the best that can be done with educational measures is to derive appropriate descriptive statistics. However, a feature of test scores is that their meaning
depends, to a large extent, on inference. This is true even for
attainment tests which are criterion-referenced, because of the
domain sampling which is necessitated (unless only a restricted domain is assessed or it is treated exhaustively; see the
discussion beginning Chapter 2, if in doubt).

To make justifiable inferences it is necessary not only to
examine test specifications (for evidence or assumptions about
pupil populations, question domains, judgement bases, the content of questions, the structure of tests and their referencing
to criteria and norms), but to relate the test data to other
educational information *of concern*. For example, the *Attitudes to Technology Questionnaire* (Page and Nash, 1980)
could, on the basis of trials and development work, be accepted
as a valid measure of four distinctive attitude viewpoints. Its
utility for general use would be strongly supported if differences in attitudes became evident between pupils in a technology oriented curriculum and pupils in an ordinary curricu-

lum. Evaluating the effect of such a curriculum would entail looking for an association between pupils' experience and their attitudes. In general, investigating associations entails examining the relationship between two variables by examining their joint interaction, as illustrated below.

Chi-square: A statistic called chi-square (Greek letter χ, pronounced 'ky') obtained by cross-classifying pupils according to attributes or test scores.

For example, in a school with 200 pupils in a year-group which has 40 pupils following a technology-based curriculum, it would be possible to classify simultaneously the pupils in two ways, that is, whether above or below the median score for an attitude variable, and whether in the ordinary curriculum group or the technology group. The cross classification would fit into a two-way tabulation as follows:

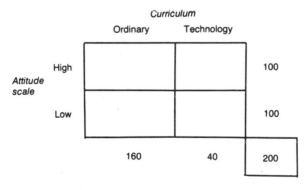

Given the distribution of pupils specified by the marginal figures, it is possible to work out how many pupils would be expected in each category cell. This is done by calculating the proportion of the total number in each cell. For example, the expected number of pupils following the *ordinary* curriculum and *above* the median attitude score is:

$$\frac{100 \times 150}{200} = 80$$

Hence the *expected frequencies* would be:

		Curriculum		
		Ordinary	Technology	
Attitude scale	High	80	20	100
	Low	80	20	100
		160	40	200

That is, the situation which would be expected if the technology curriculum had not influenced pupils' attitudes. Let us imagine that the data obtained from administering the questionnaire led to a classification as follows:

		Curriculum			
		Ordinary	Technology		
Attitude scale	High	60	40	100	Obtained frequencies
	Low	100	0	100	
		160	40	200	

This result is quite clear-cut, the whole of the Technology group belong to the higher-scoring attitude group. Hence the null hypothesis implicit in the expected frequencies is disproved unequivocally. Had this not been so evident, a test of statistical significance could be performed by calculating an index for the difference between the *observed* and *expected* frequencies, called chi-square.

Say the observed frequencies had been as follows:

Curriculum

		Ordinary	Technology	
Attitude scale	High	70	30	100
	Low	90	10	100
		160	40	200

χ^2 is calculated by finding the sum of the squared differences between observed and expected frequencies, divided by the expected frequencies, hence:

$$(O - E)$$

70 − 80 = −10	30 − 20 = 10
90 − 80 = 10	10 − 20 = −10

which with each cell difference squared, then divided by the expected frequency, gives:

$$\frac{(O - E)^2}{E}$$

$\frac{100}{80}$	$\frac{100}{20}$
$\frac{100}{80}$	$\frac{100}{20}$

which becomes:

1.25	5.0
1.25	5.0

totalling 12.5

The significance of this value for χ^2 of 12.5 has to be evaluated by referring to tables which, like t-ratios, take account of the 'degrees of freedom' to vary. For a two-by-two table, using the rule rows minus one multiplied by columns minus one (with two rows and two columns) the degrees of freedom are $(2 - 1) \times (2 - 1) = 1$. For one degree of freedom the value for χ^2 at the 1 per cent level of significance is 6.635. As 12.5 exceeds this value, the null hypothesis can be regarded as disproved. In other words, there is a very high probability that there is an association between following the Technology curriculum and more favourable attitudes towards technology.

We must be careful when interpreting this result, for an association does not necessarily show that one event caused the other, though in the absence of any other sensible explanations there may be a strong inference. But there may have been other influences, perhaps that the Technology curriculum options appealed more to pupils who enjoyed Mathematics, Science and CDT (craft, design, technology) in their previous school courses. Such a possibility could be investigated by categorizing the pupils in some other way than by curriculum followed, for example, into those keen on Mathematics, those keen on Mathematics and Science, those keen on Mathematics, Science and CDT and the remainder. In conjunction with the high-low division on the attitude scale, this categorization would give a four-by-two table; the corresponding degrees of freedom to vary for χ^2 would be $(4 - 1) \times (2 - 1) = 3$.

There is a great deal more to using χ^2 than has been indicated here. It offers a flexible method for investigating association between variables. Readers are recommended to consult a suitable text which also describes a variety of other analyses (Lewis, 1967).

Correlation: The simple two-by-two table illustrated how individuals could be cross-classified according to certain characteristics. They can also be cross-classified according to their scores on a pair of tests, to produce a *joint* frequency distribution. So in addition to the two separate distributions which show how the variation in each measure is dispersed,

Figure 6.6: **Scattergram of bi-variate distribution (N = 282)**

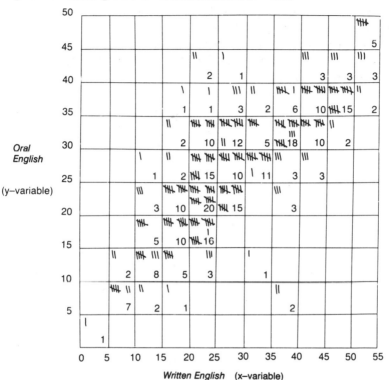

Oral English (y-variable)

Written English (x-variable)

there is also one which shows the co-variation. A scatter-plot of such a bi-variate distribution illustrates co-variation. Suppose a primary sample of pupils in an LEA had been given oral language tests and several writing tasks, with both marked in raw scores up to a maximum of 55. The results plotted on a grid with five-point class intervals might have looked like that in Figure 6.6. In this diagram each tally mark stands for an individual pupil's results. For instance, one pupil only obtained a score below 5 for each test, whilst two pupils scored between 36 and 40 for Written English but came between 6 and 10 for Oral. Also note that no one scored above 50 on the Oral test.

For each variable the respective mean x̄ and ȳ can be computed, and for each pupil the difference between score obtained and relevant variable mean can be found, that is,

$(x - \bar{x})$ and $(y - \bar{y})$. With this information in each of the 282 cases, it is possible to calculate three values, namely $(x - \bar{x})^2$, $(y - \bar{y})^2$ and $(x - \bar{x}) \times (y - \bar{y})$. When these are summed to give group totals, a ratio can be formed to indicate the degree of correlation between the two variables. The formula for this coefficient is:

$$r_{xy} = \frac{\Sigma(x - \bar{x})(y - \bar{y})}{\sqrt{[\Sigma(x - \bar{x})^2 \times \Sigma(y - \bar{y})^2}}$$

Sum of cross products divided by square root of the product of the sums of squared deviations from the two respective mean scores

With computers to hand, the extensive arithmetic entailed can be done in an instant. However, it is useful to relate the scatter in a bi-variate distribution roughly to the magnitude of the coefficient of correlation. In the plot illustrated earlier all but a few pupils' results could be enclosed in a 'fat cigar' shape, like that shown in Figure 6.7.

Figure 6.7:   Bi-variate distribution showing high co-variation

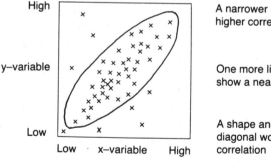

A narrower shape would show a higher correlation

One more like a circle would show a near-zero correlation

A shape angled along the other diagonal would show a negative correlation

Figure 6.8:   **Regression lines on bi-variate distribution for high and moderate correlations between x and y**

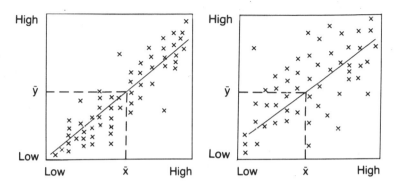

When the plot is narrow, with tallies concentrated densely along the leading diagonal, the correlation coefficient is very high, that is, between 0.9 and 1.0. In this case it is possible to talk fairly accurately of predicting a pupil's score on the y-variable from the x-variable score. When the degree of correlation is lower, it is still possible to predict a y score but with less confidence. The two diagrams in Figure 6.8 show why.

On each diagram the sloping straight line runs close to the mid-points of the vertical lines drawn through the crosses showing individual plots for x and y scores. In fact the vertical lines show the range and distribution of y scores corresponding to any x score. The high correlation *regression* line approaches an angle of 45°, whereas the lower correlation regression line has a shallower angle; for zero correlation the line would be horizontal. Hence though a score on variable y can be estimated from any given value of x, the confidence band associated with ȳ (this is derived from the standard error of estimated score) will be much wider for lower values of the coefficient. Incidentally it is possible to predict x from y, in which case a second regression line (for x upon y) could be drawn. This line would make the same angle to the y-axis as the x on y regression line makes to the x-axis. Some computer programs will produce scatter diagrams and the regression lines associated with the correlation coefficient obtained.

This description of bi-variate relationship has been given because there is a widespread notion that many tests can be used to predict a pupil's potential for scholastic attainment. The two points to appreciate in this connection are that the prediction is necessarily based on the correlation obtained for pupils in another, earlier, sample – which is then generalized to other samples; and that very high correlations between the test and the measure of achievement would be needed to predict confidently for any given pupil. A glance at the right-hand diagram in Figure 6.8 explains why. A pupil with a score of x (remember this can be any score on variable x) might be any one of those plotted on the vertical line in the scatter-plot zone.

A numerical value for an estimated score can be computed from values for the x variable mean, the SDs for variables x and y, the correlation coefficient and the score on the x variable expressed as a deviation from the mean $\bar{x}$. The formula (one of many, given other forms for the variable data) is:

$$Y_E = \bar{y} + r_{x,y} \times \frac{SD_y}{SD_x} (x - \bar{x})$$

Mean for variable y plus individual's x deviation score multiplied by the product of the correlation coefficient and the ratio of y and x variable SDs.

Example: If a mathematics standardized test and a school examination for a group of pupils give a correlation coefficient of 0.55, and respective variable data is test mean, $\bar{x}$ = 96; SDx = 12.3; examination mean, $\bar{y}$, 43; SDy, 17.1, the value of the predicted score for a pupil gaining a test score of 121 is:

$$Y_E = 43 + 0.55 \times \frac{17.1}{12.3} \times (121 - 96)$$

$$= 43 + 0.55 \times 1.39 \times 25$$

$$= 43 + 19.11$$

$$= 62.11$$

Notes: (1) The estimated score, Y_E, depends on the assumption that the regression lines, if plotted accurately, would be straight, a condition known as 'linearity'. It may seem curious to give an example of predicting a pupil's score when in fact it is already known as one of the sample of y scores. But Y_E will be close to the average y score of those pupils gaining a given x score. (2) Prediction can be done in selection procedures when a selection test score, x, is used to find a probable criterion score, Y_E, using values from previous samples in lieu of the actual y-variable data. Clearly, this method would only be defensible if the x-variable data for x̄ and SD_x had been found to be consistent on previous occasions.

For the estimated score on the predicted variable, y_E, the standard error depends on the SD of the y variable and the correlation between x and y (obtained from a previous sample). The formula for the Standard Error of Estimated Score is:

$$SE_{YE} = SD_y \ \sqrt{(1 - r^2xy)}$$

Standard deviation of the variable y multiplied by the square root of one minus the correlation coefficient squared

Example: Say variable y was assigned an SD of 9.3, and the correlation between x and y is given a value of 0.8:

$$SE_{YE} = 9.3 \times \sqrt{(1 - 0.8^2)}$$

$$= 9.3 \times \sqrt{(1 - 0.64)}$$

$$= 9.3 \times \sqrt{0.36}$$

$$= 9.3 \times 0.6 = 5.58$$

In general, the standard error of predicted scores is greater than the standard error of the predictor variable. Of course, if the expectation of predicted score level is not based on data obtained from appropriate samples of pupils, it is really too vague to evaluate. Test manuals which discuss prediction should give the data necessary for a user to gauge the size of the standard error of estimated score. Tests of ability or aptitude are often said to be capable of predicting future performance. The examples given above illustrate that prediction is seldom precise and that seemingly high correlations between predictor and subsequent criterion can only give approximate indicators for any further predictions. These points are reinforced in the discussion of expectancy tables which follows.

Expectancy tables

One method for following up test results used for guidance (that is, predictively) is to devise a table which, essentially, is a categorized bi-variate distribution. Imagine that the predicted outcome was level of external examination success and the predictor variable was a standardized composite test of reasoning ability. Using GCSE grades as the criterion in a given subject and dividing the reasoning test score range of, say, 85 to 140 into eight bands of 7 points, gives a scatter diagram as shown in Figure 6.9.

The numbers in the cells, in the figure, show how pupils tested in the second year fared in the fifth-year examination in Mathematics. There is an obvious correlation between the prior ability assessment and subsequent Mathematics examination. But for purposes of prediction it is more useful to calculate the expected outcome under the assumption that successive groups of pupils will obtain closely comparable results.

The procedure is simply to calculate the percentage likelihood of obtaining a particular grade for a corresponding test score. As the figure shows, there are a large number of cells with small numbers; it is preferable to merge adjacent cells into broader categories. If these have an educational import, so much the better. Say that a school has to decide whether to enter pupils for a high-level GCSE assessment procedure awarding A and B grades, then combining pairs of grades seems

Figure 6.9:   Example of expectancy table

		4	9	11	9	11	14	16	9	
	A					1	2	4	2	9
	B				1	2	5	0	3	11
	C					4	1	8	4	17
Maths	D		2	3	4	4	4	3		20
exam	E	1	1	4	2	4	2	1		14
grades	F	1		4		2				7
	G		1		2					3
Ungraded		2	5							7
		85–91	92–98	99–105	106–112	113–119	120–126	127–133	134–140	88

Reasoning test score

to be sensible. It also simplifies matters to combine adjacent reasoning score columns, as is shown in Figure 6.10.

With an accumulated series of results from successive years, the table could be drawn up in the original eight-by-eight format. As it stands, the expectation of obtaining either grades A or B is lower than the expectation of obtaining grades C or D for pupils whose test scores were over 126. In fact the tabulation shows that expectations with data of this order are rather imprecise. However, the only way to verify whether expectancy tables can be helpful tools is to get the data and do the tabulations. In addition, if tables were drawn up for different subjects, the utility of particular predictor variables can be evaluated.

It is worth pointing out that a great deal of 'prediction' goes on in education, though often it is not recognized as such. Examples are: setting; banding; restricted options; allocation to special education groups; access to exceptional pupils' opportunities; entry for limited grade examinations; matching pupils with the appropriate TGAT test; and, less specifically, forecasts of progress and potential in comments and reports.

Figure 6.10:   Expected grades from test scores

Test score

Grades		85–98	99–112	113–126	127–140
	A & B		1 5%	10 32%	9 39%
	C & D	2 15%	7 35%	13 42%	15 65%
	E & F	3 23%	10 50%	8 26%	1 4%
	G & Ungraded	8 62%	2 10%		
		13	20	31	23

For this cell $\dfrac{15}{23}$ = 65%

Strictly speaking, the justification for making predictions lies in the verification of predictions made on previous occasions. Expectancy tables offer a straightforward method for inferring whether or not further predictions in comparable situations are justified.

> *Exercises:* (a) Using the results for either class A or B, plot a scatter diagram showing the position of individuals jointly on Tests 1 and 2. (b) From the scatter diagram frequencies draw up an expectancy table and calculate the percentages when treating one variable as the predictor.

Making complex inferences
The heading for this section implies that the inferences described previously are not complex. This is not really the case, inferences are more or less complex as they normally involve implicit assumptions and contexts. However, when a range of data can be obtained from tests and other sources, it is natural curiosity to examine the extent to which variables interrelate, and to interpret the results inferentially.

When a sample of pupils is assessed in a number of ways, the list of their names can be accompanied by lists of several variable measures. Some measures might be test scores, others

Figure 6.11: **Illustration of matrix of relations**

	A	B	C	D	E	F	G
A	AvA	AvB	AvC	AvD	AvE	AvF	AvG
B	BvA	BvB	BvC	BvD	BvE	BvF	BvG
C	CvA	CvB	CvC	CvD	CvE	CvF	CvG
D	DvA	DvB	DvC	DvD	DvE	DvF	DvG
E	EvA	EvB	EvC	EvD	EvE	EvF	EvG
F	FvA	FvB	FvC	FvD	FvE	FvF	FvG
G	GvA	GvB	GvC	GvD	GvE	GvF	GvG

could be observation ratings or attitude scale scores. Imagine there are variables A, B, C, D, E, F and G; these can be paired in succession to give the correlation of A with B, A with C, A with D, and so on. The layout in a square matrix is given in Figure 6.11.

When the correlations for the pairs of variables are worked out the result is an *inter-correlation matrix*. In the matrix set in the figure, the values in the leading diagonal (AvA, BvB, CvC, etc.) are all 1.0 because any set of scores correlates perfectly with itself.

Furthermore, as the coefficient for AvB is the same as for BvA, and so on, it is only necessary to display inter-correlations for a set of variables in a minimal format. For example, a test manual could show the correlations for various sub-tests with the other sub-tests and teachers' ratings as in Figure 6.12. This kind of data would be obtained from trial samples of pupils. Significance levels would be indicated, and these are determined according to the sample size, by referring to the appropriate statistical table. Some computer programs incorporate the tables, and print-outs indicate conventional levels, at 5 per cent and 1 per cent, usually by printing a single or a double asterisk respectively alongside the relevant coefficient.

The high to moderate values shown in the example are typical of the results when variables which measure activities in the same curriculum area are correlated. However, had these figures come from a sample as small as ten pupils, only values over 0.6 would be significant at or beyond the 5 per cent level of significance. For a group of about 30 the value falls to almost 0.35, whilst for a group of about 100 the value is almost 0.20. In fact, though groups of pupils in particular schools would

Figure 6.12:   Inter-correlations between sub-skills and with teachers' ratings

	Sp.	Voc.	Syn.	Comp.	Fl.	Ess.	Disc.	Poe.
Spelling	–	0.8	0.7	0.5	0.6	0.8	0.5	0.2
Vocabulary		–	0.6	0.8	0.8	0.8	0.6	0.8
Syntax			–	0.7	0.4	0.7	0.2	−0.4
Comprehension				–	0.5	0.5	0.4	0.6
Fluency					–	0.7	0.6	0.3
TR Essays						–	0.3	0.4
TR Discussion							–	0.3
TR Poetry								–

not have the same characteristics as groups chosen at random from the population (because their social background and school experiences tend to make for similarities within the group), it is nevertheless helpful to examine the significance levels though the values tend to be conservative, that is, on the low side, because of the relative homogeneity.

Another way in which inter-correlations can be used is in multiple correlations, symbolized by R. Using the previous example, one question might be: 'to what extent is essay writing related to vocabulary and syntax when combined together?' In the jargon the essay score is the criterion (or dependent variable), whilst the language test sub-scores are the predictors (or independent variables).

To find R it is easier to find R^2 then to take the square root. Treating the essay score as variable 1, with the vocabulary and syntax scores as variables 2 and 3 respectively, the formula for R^2 is:

$$R^2_{1.23} = \frac{r^2_{12} + r^2_{13} - 2r_{12}r_{13}r_{23}}{1 - r^2_{23}}$$

Substituting values from the matrix (Figure 6.11), we have:

$$R^2_{1.23} = \frac{0.8^2 + 0.7^2 - 2 \times 0.8 \times 0.7 \times 0.6}{1 - 0.6^2}$$

$$= \frac{0.64 + 0.49 - 0.672}{1 - 0.36}$$

$$= \frac{1.13 - 0.672}{0.64}$$

so: $\qquad R^2 = \dfrac{0.458}{0.64} = 0.72$

hence: $\quad R = 0.85.$

The increase in association between criterion and the separate predictors is quite marked. However, it is unlikely that adding more variables to the equation would greatly enhance the degree of relationship. The reason is that, in this case, the predictor variables overlap with each other considerably, as shown by the correlation coefficients of 0.5 and over.

These days there is a trend towards more complex, computer-based tests and test analyses, though few of the techniques are novel. Teachers will find increasing use of multiple variables illustrated in the manuals and supported with case studies. One standard technique is 'multiple regression', which is an extension of multiple correlation and readily computerized. Compared with bi-variate regression, in which an estimated Y_E score is obtained from a given x score, multiple regression uses the results from a number of predictor variables, x_1, x_2, x_3 . . ., x_n to produce the estimate Y_E. The multiple regression equation has 'weights' which are coefficients applied to each pupil's predictor variable scores. Trial samples provide these data, and also a value for R^2. When this is expressed as a percentage, it shows how much of the joint variation was accounted for by the combined variables (for the group of pupils studied). The nearer the value for R^2 is to 100 per cent, the more efficient the equation. In general, multiple regression equations should only be taken seriously if the value for R^2 is in excess of 60 per cent.

Incidentally the fabricated inter-correlation matrix shown above incorporates some features which test users should look out for. One is that the sub-tests tend to correlate highly, partly because test structures tap similar attributes (some children enjoy a test and so do well, others sink dismally). A batch of high inter-correlations also implies that the sub-tests are not neatly differentiating between attributes to any great extent, as far as pupil measurement is concerned. Another feature is that the teachers' ratings tend to exhibit low inter-correlation. This happens when several teachers are involved and their criteria are not standardized.

An unusual part of the example matrix is the negative correlation introduced between Syntax and Poetry. This is an exception to the otherwise positive values throughout the table. On occasion inter-correlation matrices are subjected to a technique called 'factor analysis' (Child, 1970), which draws out the dimensions which underlie the relationships between the variables. Had the Syntax vs Poetry correlation been positive, a further analysis might have revealed a single dimension of 'language attainment'. But the single negative value might have led to a smaller factor, for an attribute which might be interpreted as 'poeticism', in which vocabulary, fluency and poor syntax would combine.

Readers of test manuals should be less impressed by high correlations between sub-tests than by high correlations with criteria which interest them. Test validation by comparison with other tests is less convincing than validation done with measures obtained from school situations (more aptly, the situations in which tests will be used in relation to a specific purpose).

This chapter has dealt fairly explicitly with a few of the methods which may be used for examining and applying test results. Recent advances in using programs in computers has made the techniques far more accessible, leaving the logistics of data entry as the major problem in utilization. Chapter 7 describes some test construction methods, with the aim of showing how good-quality tests are developed.

CHAPTER 7
Test Development Methods

This chapter is intended to give an outline of the methods used to develop tests and some other forms of assessment. Sound test development entails careful thought and well organized development work. A test manual should contain evidence of how the test was devised, and the user should look for this information so as to take it into account when judging the quality and aptness of a test. Furthermore, during an era when teachers will increasingly have to devise their own curricular assessments to use alongside SATs or in the intervening key-stage periods, some of the procedures could be helpful. The reasons for this are twofold: (i) the assessment would have an explicit basis, and (ii) they could be justified or defended in a rational way.

Some of the concepts which bear on test construction have been discussed in previous chapters, particularly those which relate to populations of pupils or questions and the types of tests and testing applications. Here we take these into account whilst focusing on techniques and procedures. Their relevance to other forms of assessment and the manner in which they could be used are then considered.

Outline of stages

State purpose – say what attribute it is intended to assess, together with the population it will suit and how the results could or should be used.

Define rationale – justify the basis for the judgements arising from the attribute measured by the test items or tasks performed by a pupil, referring to a score or criterion; give a detailed analysis of a curriculum, a theory of learning or characteristic behaviour; hypothesize links between the assessment result and the pupils' current state or future learning, or their present difficulties, or describe applications in particular circumstances; also say how scores or other kinds of results should be interpreted (for example, via criteria, norms, theory-based categories).

Consider differentiation – show how differences between pupils will be generated. In many tests the pupils are separated by outcome (that is, a range of scores will span all possible population outcomes). In some tests and examinations pupils are matched to tasks chosen from ascending stages; this is differentiation according to task. In the latter case, it is crucial to specify how individual pupils will be matched with the task appropriate to their development when the assessment is to be made.

Decide on question types – choose objective-type (multiple-choice, matching, completion), open-ended or supply-type (for example, pupils complete a task, calculate, draw, write freely to structured headings, solve problems, construct an article, write for an audience, design or compose creatively), or performance for adjudication by an observer.

Design format – specify the lay-out of printed matter (instructions, questions, mark schemes, criteria schedules, record sheets, task descriptions, administration guides for teachers and technical data); use of photographs, video, apparatus, computers; say how pupils and teachers should make use of the various parts of the assessment.

Find tasks or questions – identify sources such as textbooks, curriculum guides, teachers' groups, examiners; write or describe test items or assessment situations designed to reflect the rationale, using the appropriate question types and formats; produce more questions than specified in test structure; carry out critical review (to discard or amend flawed items).

Try out tasks or questions – arrange trials with small samples of pupils; specify instructions for administrators and pupils; write score or classification keys and provide examples or oral prompts for inter-active assessments (when teachers have a dialogue with the pupil being assessed).

Analyse and scrutinize pupils' responses – the numbers of pupils giving each response option or classified response should be counted and tabulated as a distribution; open-ended responses should be classified or graded and the distributions tabulated; when markers or examiners use their own judgements to score or classify, conduct cross checks for consistency (inter-judge reliability).

Check for bias – three kinds of bias may be evident: (i) in the content of test items whereby matters more familiar to males (for example, fishing, trains) or a particular ethnic group predominate; (ii) appearance (for example, females portrayed in sexist situations, no ethnic minorities in the illustrations); and (iii) inter-group variations in proportions obtaining correct answers or overall test statistics for reliability and validity (any differences should be examined; they might reveal undetected biases of the first two kinds or be judged to represent group differences adequately/badly). A further source of bias with open-ended response items lies in the adjudicator's perceptions and values; these should be addressed through cross check exercises and discussion.

Hold large-scale trials (for published tests or material destined for wide substantial usage) – obtain suitable representative sample (for example, 3000 pupils drawn from 100 schools); train teachers in administration and scoring, if necessary; give test and analyse results tabulating distributions and carrying out item by item analyses (see next section); examine inter-judge reliability; specify and collect related data for validity check study.

Edit items and other materials – use trial data and users' comments to produce final versions of tasks or tests, scoring guides, instructions for administration and how to arrange for machine scoring, if utilized.

Finalize scoring system – produce the key for obtaining raw scores (for example, numbers of items correct or points awarded for an essay, a sketch or live performance); detail methods for transferring to other scales (for example, percentile ranks, scaled scores, percentages, progress indicators,

TGAT levels or for employing the pupil's response to categorize it).

Provide for reports – layout record forms or profiles, with aids to score interpretation and indications of the standard error(s) or other limits users should apply.

Illustrate interpretations of results – consider what a score or classification means; can it be generalized to a learning domain (such as attainment target level, a personal attribute, comparable situations or individual performances); how can predictions be calculated (or made using tables)? Here the validity study data from the trials can be used in a case study showing how the assessment can serve a stated purpose.

Evaluate – examine the whole test and assessment procedure in relation to purposeful use; indicate sensible limitations, especially in the rationale and interpretations claimed; clarify and state the training and knowledge required of the user to obtain valid interpretations of the results.

Produce the test and manual – edit text, print material; assemble other components; package ready for distribution.

It is instructive to look at some recently published test materials to see whether the evidence of sound methods has been provided. *Touchstones: Cross Curricular Group Assessments* (Jones *et al.*, 1989) were a rapidly developed response to the TGAT recommendation to test pupils at about the age of seven. Taking the headings discussed above as a checklist gives one procedure for evaluating the materials; the outcome is set out below.

State purpose: The Introduction refers to the TGAT structure of ten levels and cites national assessment as serving both formative and summative ends. In a section called 'Purpose' two main objectives are given: (i) to assess children over a range of attainment targets drawn from English, Mathematics, and Science and Technology, specified for the first key stage; and (ii) to assist teachers with developing their own skills in assessing children.

Define rationale: A very brief passage (which refers to the comparative nature of norm referenced tests) states the basis as criterion referenced. 'Pupil performance is measured against defined criteria.' There are 10 thematic pupils' activity booklets, but these are to give teachers flexibility to choose one or more themes. The tasks prompted by the activities booklets may be done in groups of 4 to 6 children working together or individually, in settings which resemble good learning situations in normal primary classrooms.

Differentiation: As Levels 1, 2, 3 and 4 are dealt with for each reporting subject, differentiation is relative to a particular theme criterion written for each level within each attainment target. The criteria describe task activity (for example, Estimates length and width of longest and shortest feathers in cm). Though differentiation is effected by judging a child's performance in relation to a theme criterion, each theme booklet and task does not cover all of the attainment targets. Hence, to differentiate children in respect of every attainment target in the core reporting subjects, it would be necessary to give an individual child at least six of the ten booklets. A further aspect is that the four levels appropriate to pupils at the end of Key Stage One are not covered entirely whenever an attainment target is assessed; for example, Mathematics AT4 Estimation, is dealt with in two theme booklets, but in each one only level 3 is assessed.

Decide on question types: Each theme booklet has a sequence of task instructions followed by questions, which the child responds to by writing short answers, or more extended pieces, or by drawing, or speaking (these are supply-type items).

Design format: For each theme there is an Activity Booklet, an Individual Profile referenced to AT levels and a Group Assessment Booklet (that is, a group record form). All are clearly printed and laid out. The Activity Booklets have different sections for the various activities specified and ample space for pupils' written answers. In addition, the record charts contain guidance notes and spaces for dates, teacher's initials, and comments. The format and printing of all of the material is of an exemplary standard.

Find tasks or questions: The activities were developed co-operatively by a test development team and two groups of teachers in separate counties. The different topics (that is, themes) were written by individual authors.

Try-out tasks: The teachers involved in developing the theme activities booklets and assessments carried out informal trials.

Analyse pupils' responses: Results from the informal trials are not given in the manual (NB – this is usually the case).

Check for bias: The test materials were reviewed for biased content and illustrative material; no data analyses for identified subgroups are given.

Hold large-scale trials: Two samples of pupils were drawn; one from schools in the two development authorities which had not previously been involved; the other was a stratified representative sample from other authorities. In all there were 711 seven-year-olds; a second sample of 294 eight-year-olds (1st year juniors) was also given test activities. About a half of these numbers also completed a second activity booklet. The data showing the numbers or proportions of pupils credited with reaching or surpassing each attainment target level is not given. What is displayed are tables showing examples of (a) reliability within a task activity and (b) reliability between task activities. There are contingency tables showing the numbers of children gaining congruent levels or otherwise when (a) they attempted two questions for the same attainment target in a theme booklet; or (b) they attempted two questions for the same attainment tasks in different theme booklets. Validity has been addressed in terms of match between the task activities and attainment targets as judged by the test constructors and teachers who reviewed the materials.

Edit items and other materials: The activities booklets and supporting materials were reviewed and revised prior to eventual publication.

Finalize scoring system: The Marking System has four categories indicated by a tick for *level attained*, a horizontal arrow for *level almost attained*, a cross for *level not attained*, and a circle for *unable to assess level*. These symbols can be recorded in the Group Assessment Booklet (showing results for up to six children who have worked together at a theme booklet) and on the Pupil Profile (which is specific for each theme).

Provide for reports: The scoring and recording systems also have space for teachers' comments; for example, that a particular pupil was given alternative (easier) questions so as not to discourage. Interventions of this kind are part of the skill needed for administration but they should be noted.

Illustrate interpretations: There are two separate parts concerned with interpretation: one deals with assessing English. There are guidelines on how to judge pupils' responses to the tasks which also indicate how these may be interpreted. The second part is about the reliability of assessments of this kind when only a single question or a small number of questions are used to assess an attainment target. The contingency tables illustrate that some unreliability is to be expected when individual pupils are assessed. It is pointed out in the manual that more secure interpretations can be had when a pupil attempts more than one set of activities (that is, works through two or three theme booklets which address the same attainment targets). Inspection of the theme coverage of ATs shows that, except for English, achieving this amount of coverage is not possible in a number of cases.

Of course, the examination of the test materials should include the items, but these seldom have obvious flaws. As the comments given above show, the materials evaluation goes only so far. Any thorough evaluation of a test should include an account of making use of it. This would highlight not only the adequacy of matters such as clarity of administration instructions and so on; more critically, an explanation of validity in genuine operational settings is made available and these data are more important than the rest.

At first reading, the evaluation comments given above appear mainly factual. There is no judgement offered about the suitability of the test materials, even though the layout and presentation has been commended. There is, however, an inherent judgement because when little has been said under the checklist headings, the test quality must be suspect.

Teachers developing tests or assessments

Much of the assessment of pupils' curricular progress should be carried out informally by teachers during the course of lessons; and some assessment can be done by pupils themselves when they have suitable guidance. Indeed, one aspect of promoting learning is pupils acquiring assessment know-how. So course objectives and criteria for differentiating/judging the work done should form part of the curriculum. With older pupils, this can be formalized; for example, by giving a class the aims for a term's work or for a module. In some settings, pupils may assess each other at a range of tasks, leaving the teacher to check key attainments periodically.

Involving pupils in assessing their peers exemplifies the need for having a structured approach. For example, in a French lesson, one pupil in a pair used a cue sheet to ask questions prompting the use of vocabulary in the context of buying clothes. The *purpose* was clearly stated as communicating which articles might be purchased, inquiring the prices of each and buying a garment. The *rationale* was that accuracy was the basis, because it is important to understand what something will cost before it is bought; to reinforce this point, each pupil was prompted 'to buy' five articles. *Differentiation* related to the number of 'correct' replies: four or five correct meant going to the teacher for a further test and another set of questions; fewer than four meant practising and asking for help. The *question types* were supply rather than open-ended, as the cues tended to prompt a standard form of answer. However, the more fluent pupils were encouraged to try to use their skills, and the teacher–test extended this aspect deliberately by awarding a bonus point. The cue sheet *design format* represented a huge investment in time by the teachers, as it was one of the ways in which the curriculum was linked with assessment. There were photographs, signs, posters and labels as well as text in French and English. Heavy type and devices such as boxes showed pupils what should be read aloud and what to listen for. There was a series of *tasks* determined in part by the content of the commercial course chosen by the department and in part by the LEA's proficiency test level. The tasks and questions had been developed through *try-outs* with pupils during which teachers observed pupils' responses and their application of criteria. The data on year-groups was summarized, that is, *analysed,* for the check tests given by the teacher. The *validity* of the tests was verified by the high pass rate when pupils took the LEA's graded assessment (though this would be expected). The *records and reports* were catered for by pupils keeping a chart showing the peer tests and check test results; teachers had class charts showing the results from the range of check tests for a number of topics. The extent to which pupils gained a satisfactory score on a range of topics gave *interpretations* of progress through the scheme as a whole.

This scheme of criterion-referenced proficiency tests showed also that the pupils and teachers needed to have training in its use and practice to become familiar with the administration rules and record sheets. When a class was observed, it was evident that the twelve-year-old pupils took their role of testers and recorders very seriously. Pupils can also assess themselves, given guidance and practice, as a national modern language assessment project (Lee and Dickson, 1989) illustrates. In this project several groups of teachers tackled several themes, such as what to assess and why; how to assess effectively in classrooms. A self-assessment sheet from Kent shows nine circles laid out in three rows of three, with criteria couched as 'I can . . .' statements underneath, and a scoring system at the foot of the page. Each circle represents an 'Exercise'; the circles are divided into six sectors labelled 'understanding', 'fluency', 'message', 'accuracy', 'pronunciation' and 'extra'. The latter shows that the pupil judges him/herself as capable of introducing additional dialogue and taking the initiative.

The publication, *Assessment in Action*, is a guide to teacher groups on how to formulate and develop assessments for classrooms and school schemes. It draws on teacher group experiences by suggesting activities which may be productive; these concern From Principles to Practice; Classroom Assessment; Developing an Approach; Speaking – Choice of Criteria; Speaking – Scoring and Using Results; Listening and Reading – Texts for Assessment; Listening and Reading – Tasks for Assessment; Listening and Reading – Organization; Writing – Choice of Task; Writing – Organizational Procedures, and Classroom Assessment and School Schemes. Much of the practice the authors recommend to teachers is appropriate to assessment in the general sense because it relies on the teacher's observation of individual pupils whilst moving about the room, or their subsequent judgement of written productions.

From the examples cited and the test development routines described before them, it is possible to envisage how teachers might go about reliably assessing pupils on progress in the National Curriculum without resorting to 'clipboard teaching'. The first point is that working in teacher-groups has advantages, the main one being that ideas can be brainstormed collectively and these form the basis for further ideas. The second point is that *a single purpose* should be agreed upon. Perhaps 'To determine pupils' levels of proficiency at national attainment targets in the core and foundation reporting subjects' is sufficiently crisp. Note that there is no mention of any other purpose, such as diagnosis, which is discussed later.

The next step, conceptualizing a *rationale*, is an exercise in problem-solving. What to assess level by level has been or will be laid down, usually in general terms. Hence, the central question is how? One suggestion is to work towards a combination of classrooms and classroom or school tests. Remember that assessments other than tests arise from the work in hand, whereas tests require a stimulus task and a judgement framework. Possibly the most critical aspect of the TGAT scheme is that the 10 levels are, notionally, progressive in two-year stages from the age of 5 years; the exceptions are the lower or higher attainers. Hence, the steps between the levels are relatively large; fine distinctions are not required. However, a fair degree of accuracy in differentiation (that is, reliability) is desirable, as teachers would be hardpressed to justify inconsistent results to parents.

A mistake which afflicted some records of achievement developments was to attempt to observe and record virtually every aspect of achievement for each pupil. When the burden of recording was shared with the pupils, who kept grids or charts gummed into exercise books or folders, the welter of forms was reduced to a small number of summary records (occasionally maintained on disks). Another factor is the timing of national tests. For the school year-groups affected, it is likely that the period between Easter and Whitsuntide will be the one when schools are engaged in testing pupils. Hence, for the year-groups involved, a teacher's own recorded assessments will have to be finished by Easter.

So that schools do not become confused – or confuse parents – about what they are doing, it is suggested that a school assessment programme is laid out. For an infant and junior school, the programme might look like this:

	Autumn	Spring	Summer	
Year 1	CA		CA	5–6 year olds
Year 2		TA	SATs	6–7 year olds
Year 3		CA		7–8 year olds
Year 4	ST		CA	8–9 year olds
Year 5		ST		9–10 year olds
Year 6		TA	SATs	10–11 year olds

KEY CA = Class Assessments   TA = Teacher Assessments
     ST = School Tests

Between the recorded assessments, this scheme allows for at least one term of uninterrupted teaching, during which assessment would be focused entirely on diagnostic appraisal and coaching. Note that there is no proposal to test five-year-olds or younger children shortly after entry to the school. With the class assessments to be done in December, organizing the traditional festivities might be seen to by parents or other volunteers!

The initial class assessments in December could deal with *vocabulary*, in the context of early reading, speaking and listening, and writing; *physical control*, for body mobility and control of tools (pens, pencils, scissors); *aspects of number* (for example, counting, ordering, grouping), simple computation and the representation of numerals in writing, speech and diagrams; *using materials*, tools and equipment; *observing*, when handling and describing natural and man-made objects; and *musical activities* including singing. Many schools have records similar to those listed above, and it is common practice for teachers to keep a diary as an aide-mémoire which relates how children developed in their learning activities. A great deal of information reaches parents through the 'work' that children take home, too. This semi-formal communication can and should continue as a natural outcome of classroom activity. Basically, then, the December assessment by teachers should be treated as a developmental summary, couched in terms that suit the class curriculum.

These early assessments should be neither exhaustive nor extensive, but concerns raised by teachers or voiced by parents should be noted. Also, factors bearing on a child's work at school should be recorded (any physical or mental conditions), and any particular attainments should be described briefly. Discussion with parents should be factual, for example, 'This is an outline of how we see your child's development; it's a snapshot of progress so far'. Predictions and comments on personal characteristics should not enter into consideration, though parents should be made aware that their interest and encouragement will help. There is a good case, too, for having a space for a written parent's remark on the record sheet; this will establish the 'open' nature of the record and give any parent an opportunity to draw attention to concerns which should be addressed.

The second assessment at around Whitsuntide in Year 1 would also be based on the class curriculum – hence the use of the term class assessment – but by this time the National Curriculum programmes of study will have been taken into account. In contrast with the initial assessment, projects or topics and scheme-based work will provide the situations for assessments. Primary school teachers tend to worry that they have not been trained in assessing, especially the age-group they teach at present. By and large, their involvement with children as they work promotes the skills they require, principally observation and prompting. What they then need is an approach which fits into the classroom situation and a structure which facilitates the task.

As in the case of *Touchstones*, the structure can readily be derived from the National Curriculum attainment targets. The rationale suggested is that the assessments should be confined solely to Level 1. At this stage most parents would accept that a check on the introduction of the National Curriculum is desirable. The measurement 'scale' would be a simple 'Yes' or 'No', standing for 'Yes; this pupil is judged to be working at or above Level 1', or 'No; this pupil is judged not to be working at Level 1'. At this juncture, the fundamental assessment skills are (i) producing learning situations which prompt children into activities which map onto the assessment agenda (that is, Level 1 ATs); this can be done by planning topics, projects, investigations or activities incorporating one or more assessment situations; and (ii) interacting with the individual children to observe what they do rather than to explain or demonstrate or extend by questioning. In other words, teaching to promote understanding is suspended during assessing in favour of prompting a child to show his or her particular capabilities.

In preliminary work with practical mathematics assessments (Kyles and Sumner, 1977) it was found that teachers needed to practise how to keep their teaching skills in suspense. Otherwise, they tended to give information or strong cues to pupils. One way in which this was done was to ask a question, then shortly afterwards to give an answer if the pupil had not done so. Apart from concentrating on observing individual pupils, teachers' questions should be aimed at eliciting information or activity; e.g. 'Can you tell me . . .' and 'Can you show me . . .?'.

The Year 1 Summer Class Assessments can be used as the starting point for the Year 2 Spring TAs, which precede the SATs. Again, the main vehicle for assessments should be teacher's observation or children's class work. Teachers' major concern will be to plan how to map the projects or topics onto the Key Stage programmes of study which allow the more advanced children to work at Levels 2 and 3. The SEAC has decided that the lower attaining pupils will be assessed as 'in Level 1', so this must be the lowest of the levels considered.

Class records could be arranged to give straightforward analyses describing the progress of groups within the class by attainment targets. For example:

| | | *Spring Year 2* | | |
		No. at Level 1	No. at Level 2	No. at or above Level 3
Summer Year 1	No. not yet working at Level 1	a	c	e
	No. at or above level 1	b	d	f
Class profile Spring Year 2		a + b	c + d	e + f

Clearly, the pupils in cell b would be of particular concern, as there would be no development to report (given that the assessments were infallible – hardly likely). Indeed, we would hope for a zero in cell b; any pupils who remained in it after due consideration should certainly be discussed to see whether a special needs procedure should be initiated. This would, of course, depend on the results from the SATs given in the following term. These would modify the class profile and provide some feedback on the validity of the TAs.

The rationale for the Year 3 Class Assessments, once more, could be that they are based on the class curriculum *at the time*. Consequently, the teachers' observations would relate only to a limited set of attainment targets for Key Stage 2, that is, those relevant to each pupil's work. By this time, it is possible that some children will have developed certain attainments more rapidly than other pupils, so record sheets would have to be designed to accommodate higher-level criteria, as well as a range of attainment targets within subjects. The School Tests, in the Autumn term of Year 4, could be focused on attainment targets which are less readily covered in normal classwork. As the *Touchstones* package illustrates very well, pupils produce a great deal of writing, in English and other curricular contexts; so there should be no need whatever to set up a writing task; similarly for reading.

An alternative use for the School Tests slot would be to give the year-group a standardized test, as indicated later on in Chapter 10 (with a purposeful design, as described in Chapter 9). If this were done the Class Assessment in the Summer term of Year 4 could then be used to appraise more of the less commonly experienced attainment targets. Also, the School Test could be used for either a year-group based attainment target test or assessment or for a standardized test appropriate to the school's information needs.

If a school were to design a test in a subject, such as Mathematics, with rationale aimed at the assessment of a set of attainment targets and levels, procedures akin to those described earlier in this chapter would be useful. For example, a test with questions or tasks pitched at levels 2, 3 and 4 for five attainment targets would, as a minimum, require fifteen items. Bearing in mind that single items can hardly yield a reliable result, it would be better to have forty-five. Of course, it would not be necessary to have all these questions done by the pupils at one time; by adopting a module as a standard pattern, and using, say, two modules in each of three weeks, four or five items can be set for each level. An earlier study, into assessment for transition from primary to secondary school, found that such short, three-level tests (four items at each level) could be highly reliable (Sumner and Bradley, 1977).

The term 'School Tests' has been used to emphasize that whatever is done by way of formal assessment, there should be a school policy embodying a clear aim, and the basis should be the whole year-group, not each teacher's class. In larger schools, this would represent a team effort with data on results shared between teachers; in this way, common features and appropriate differences could be appreciated. Various tasks could be distributed, for example, checking for gender or ethnic bias in the content, and inter-marker comparisons could be made when open-ended responses are judged in relation to criteria.

The national government's intention to make schools report to parents on each child's attainments with respect to the curricular targets makes it imperative that schools have sound assessment methods and materials. Once these are developed, they could be kept for a period of time; being improved by adaptation rather than replaced. The analysis of data, as suggested in the grid given above, would provide one source of information whether the methods are satisfactory.

For secondary schools, a pattern of assessment that allows for an initial analysis of the intake of pupils is essential. Schools with pupils aged 11–16 years might consider a system such as the one shown below.

	Autumn	Spring	Summer	
Year 7	Intake analysis		CA	11–12 year olds
Year 8		ST		12–13 year olds
Year 9		TA	SATs	13–14 year olds
Year 10			ST	14–15 year olds
Year 11			GCSE	15–16 year olds

KEY CA = Class Assessments   TA = Teacher Assessments
    ST = School Tests

Here, the purpose of the Year 8 school tests (for example, the modular type set to cover several levels) would be to give a basis for changing pupils' sets (if these are the teaching groups), before the start of Year 9. The Year 10 school tests would replace the traditional mock 16 plus examinations. Many schools would be reluctant to abandon these, but the alternative would be to carry out teacher assessment in the Summer of Year 10 and do mocks late in the Autumn or early Spring terms.

Whereas the class assessments at the end of Year 7 would be based on the observations teachers make of pupils working at the current attainment targets, the school tests would be more formal. Because year-groups may by this time have become highly differentiated in relation to subject attainment targets, the curriculum departments might need a set of differentiated tests. These could be modular and structured so as to give overlaps, for example, Module A, levels 3, 4, 5; Module B, levels 5, 6, 7; Module C, levels 7, 8, 9. As course-work is an important part of the GCSE assessment, it should also be part of the preceding ones. However, the case for devising and setting school tests rests on the same argument (unfortunately, perhaps), that is, that all GCSEs have a test as part of the assessment.

The emphasis which the National Curriculum has placed on attainment assessment and the requirement for annual reports on attainment target progress means that schools may not find the time or inclination to assess pupils' abilities. In the writer's view, this is regrettable, as past experience has shown how useful information on these attributes can be, for certain pupils, both for class teachers and for specific educational guidance. However, it is re-iterated that, when teachers devise their own tests or assessments, they work in collaboration with a colleague in following similar development stages to those outlined at the beginning of this chapter. This may benefit from some technical work when pupils' responses are looked at in more detail.

Item analysis

Test users should expect to find information in manuals about the analyses made of data about pupils' responses to the questions. Trials with carefully drawn representative samples of pupils furnish two kinds of information. One relates to each item as an entity, the other relates each item to the test as a whole. Both are really about how the *pupils* responded as a group, though test constructors have a reprehensible habit of talking about how an 'item behaved'.

The first statistic to be calculated is the percentage of the sample to give a correct response; and if there are multiple options, the percentages choosing each one. The percentage correct is called the 'item facility value'. It is useful for a number of reasons, primarily because the facility value allows the constructor to gauge the item in relation to the pupil population and the test blueprint. For instance, if a complex trigonometry question with multiple-choice answer options had a facility of 77 per cent when tried out with a sample of fourth year secondary pupils, the item would be closely scrutinized to see whether there were obvious reasons for an unexpectedly good result. Perhaps a diagram prompted good guesses because the perspective made one line 'look right' (and this was the correct response). Judgements of the kind described must be made circumspectly because even panels of subject experts (teachers, the HMI, advisers) have been found to be widely astray when asked to estimate facility values before trials have been completed.

The second main item statistic is called the 'discrimination index'. This is obtained by calculating a ratio or a correlation coefficient, which shows the extent to which the pattern of correct/incorrect responses agreed with the high to low distribution of total scores. A rather dated method for obtaining a discrimination index is to arrange the trial sample of pupils in descending order according to total score, and then to divide these into those ranked in the upper third, those in the middle band and those ranked in the lowest third. Facility values for the three bands are then calculated item by item. Examples of how a few results in percentages might appear are:

	item 1	item 5	item 18	item 50
Upper third	86	73	30	37
Middle third	70	55	55	23
Lower third	60	32	40	4
Difference between upper and lower thirds	26	41	−10	33

However, because this is an index, the results are expressed as a proportion, that is, 0.26, 0.41, −0.10 and 0.33.

Nowadays the pupils' item responses are dealt with by computer programs which calculate an appropriate correlation coefficient as an index of discrimination. As the example illustrates, positive values show that an item makes a contribution to the discrimination achieved by the test through the total score. A negative value shows that the item responses contradict the general run – something is amiss, so the item is discarded.

These statistics are usually supplemented by others; for instance, the total score obtained by all of the pupils who give a particular response can be shown. The implied relationship here is that lower-scoring pupils will give higher proportions of incorrect answers. However, in a multiple-choice test the distribution of responses between all of the options is of interest. Clearly, if one option attracts a high proportion of erroneous answers whilst another attracts very few, the latter option is contributing little to the discrimination between pupils given by that item. Item analysis along these lines is carried out to improve the quality of the test items and the test as a whole.

In norm-referenced tests it is usual to choose items with a range of facility values, from relatively easy to relatively hard, and also to only use items that discriminate efficiently. These would yield indices usually over a value of 0.4 for the upper minus lower method, or 0.3 when a correlation coefficient is used. The technical terms 'facility' and 'discrimination' often appear in manuals when authors write a section on 'test development'. When the data is summarized it indicates to prospective users something of the quality of the separate items in the test.

The methods described above are usually referred to as 'classical' or 'traditional' because the basic premise is that a test must discriminate effectively between the pupils who take it. Whilst this premise is readily accepted for norm-referenced tests, it is less obvious for proficiency or criterion-referenced tests or for diagnostic tests. However, unless a test has the *potential* for discriminating about something, it can do little to inform educational decision-making, that is, it cannot serve any kind of purpose.

For tests which measure performance relative to a criterion

(in a skills and knowledge domain) it is clear that discrimination can be assessed in relation to the specific criterion defined. One example is the use of three levels in a set of ten mathematics modular tests designed to convey information to the secondary teachers about individual children's attainments at the end of the primary stage of schooling (Sumner and Bradley, op. cit.). Each module had 12 questions, four pitched at each level, with boundaries at scores 4/5 and 8/9. In this case an index similar to the upper and lower thirds method could be obtained. This was based on the proportions answering an item correctly for those pupils whose total score placed them in one or other of the levels, for example:

	item 1	item 2	item 7	item 12
Upper level (scores 9–12)	1.00	0.9	0.9	0.8
Middle level (scores 5–8)	1.00	0.8	0.5	0.2
Lower level (scores 0–4)	0.8	0.8	0.2	0.0
difference (U – M)	0.0	0.1	0.4	0.6
difference (M – L)	0.2	0.0	0.3	0.2
difference (U – L)	0.2	0.1	0.7	0.8

Here, the discrimination indices are calculated for the criterion decision points (hence, we are looking at *criterion-referenced validity*). Compared with the previous results, judgements about the usefulness of the items would be quite different. In a norm-referenced test an index as low as 0.2 would be regarded as too low for the item to be included in a final test draft. Whereas in the situation where the criterion is pupil learning reflected by the item, low discrimination can be quite acceptable; indeed, from a teacher's point of view, this result could be ideal, provided that the facility value (overall percentage correct) is very high. This outcome would be very acceptable for attainment target based tests, even though 'norms' are stipulated by linking certain levels with particular ages. The distributions of pupils across the levels will indicate whether the assessments have functioned as discriminators in the technical sense outlined here. By the same token, an item with a low discrimination index and low facility value may be acceptable, depending on the composition of the criterion domain and the nature of the sample of pupils given the test.

This point is quite crucial. If a criterion-referenced test is designed to show whether a group of pupils following a course have 'mastered' it, the discrimination ought to show up when the test is given to a group of similar pupils who have not taken the course. Naturally it would be bizarre to give, say, a test of speaking Russian to a group of pupils who have never studied the language. However, it is reasonable to examine how test items discriminate between pupils who have followed the same course whose tutors nominate some as 'proficient' (or in mastery-learning contexts, as 'masters'). Also, in this case an index can be calculated based on the comparison between the two groups. Another way of harnessing judges' opinions is to ask a large group of teachers or others with knowledge of the attribute tested to say which items in a test draft a proficient pupil would answer correctly. In this case an index showing degree of judges' unanimity is used to decide which items are likely to be effective.

A more complex method of analysing items, mentioned in Chapter 5, is to place each one on a scale of relative difficulty, provided that consistency is found between the items when different samples of pupils are compared. In practice, a single sample of pupils can be given a draft test and then be divided into arbitrary groups, such as the high-scorers and low-scorers (see Wright and Stone, 1979, for routine procedures for one method originally proposed by Rasch). The results, give or take variations due to random error (significant according to sample size) should be very similar for the two groups when a constant is introduced to compensate for the relative 'ability' of the samples.

Item selection

The items tried out in test drafts are used as a pool from which final versions are assembled. Users should find information in manuals about how items were selected to produce a set for the test which fulfils the rationale effectively. It is clear from the different types of item analyses mentioned, whatever the method of item analysis, the results are used to improve on the drafts. For example, if two equivalent forms of a test are stipulated, they are matched for overall level of difficulty as well as being structured in the same way for content and format. So from perhaps four drafts of 85 items each, two second drafts of 80 items will be compiled. These will have similar facility values, item by item through the tests. Then a second round of trials, again with sample of pupils drawn from the target population, will be held to produce item-response data which will be analysed using the same methods as before.

When two forms of a test are constructed, the extent to which the pairs of tests generate comparable results (raw score distributions and comparable ranks for pairs of items) is investigated. Usually the trial sample of pupils is divided into two sub-samples using a simple randomization procedure. For example, the test booklets have different colours for the front sheets and teachers are asked to give alternate pupils a different colour. Test manuals should give a summary of the data on equivalence of results from comparable samples. Users should look critically at the methods used *and* any data given to see whether they were appropriate, in that the forms of the test are genuinely interchangeable. This information will be important in the case of SATs when teachers are allowed to choose whichever versions they feel are most suitable.

It is most unusual for properly conducted trials to produce inconsistent item analysis results. There will, naturally, be some variation between the facility values for items even when they have not been modified between successive trials. However, using the data available, the test developer assembles the final version of the test(s). Again the rationale is paramount. Three examples will illustrate the point.

First, consider a 'general ability' test with sub-sections for a range of reasoning tasks intended for LEA surveys. Items for a test of this kind have to suit the pupil population at large, across the extremes of the distribution. Hence item facilities must have a broad range, and this usually runs from as low as 10 per cent up to 90 per cent. For a test intended for one age-group the bulk of the items will be concentrated in the 25 per cent to 75 per cent band. A test intended for several age-groups will have item facilities evenly graduated to suit the span of the age range.

In contrast, consider a test designed to select the hypothetically most able 5 per cent of pupils. There is little point in using large numbers of relatively easy items as these would not discriminate between pupils in the upper end of the distribution. Hence only items with low facility values are selected.

Lastly, consider a proficiency test in speaking a foreign language in a simulated real-life situation. Item trial data might be used to give a test consisting of questions principally which only pupils judged to be proficient will answer correctly. In this case facility values would be ignored, whilst the analyses for discrimination between criterion groups would be used. However, because such a test might appear extremely artificial, a more authentic task could be chosen as a setting for the questions, with marking confined solely to the discriminating items.

It is stressed, again, that prospective test users should look for information about item analyses in manuals, or write asking for data to test publishers whenever it is relevant to the choice of a test.

Standardization

As pointed out in earlier chapters, there are two aspects of standardization. One is the uniformity of materials administration and scoring (or classifying pupils' responses); the other is securing data on population standards as shown by test performance. The first aspect is important for tests of all kinds, whether norm referenced, proficiency or criterion-performance referenced, or diagnostic.

If data which relates to a population is required, the final test version (or versions) is administered to a representative sample or several samples. Nowadays for some types of test it is considered useful to have test standardizations for different times of the school year, either termly or before and after a transfer point, say, in June and October. For selection tests, standardization is timed to suit the administrative timetable. February used to be the favoured month, but with LEAs today having to allow time for parented appeals November is also used. Even though one age-group is tested at a particular time, it is possible to extend the standardization tables to cover up to 16 months by extrapolating age allowances by two or three months each way. Anyone thinking of using a test should examine age-score tables to ensure that the age range of pupil to be tested fits into the limits as tabulated.

When two parallel or equivalent versions of a test are being standardized to produce norms, the most satisfactory method is for the same group of children to do both tests. One way of doing this, to take account of practice effects from the first occasion and increased capability arising from the time difference, is to give half of the sample version A and the other half version B on the first occasion and then exchange versions for the second occasion four to six weeks later.

Yet another sub-sample can be given the same version of the test on both occasions. Hence data are available for reliability studies of internal consistency (if appropriate), the stability of scores over time and equivalence of score values between forms of the test. Again manuals should supply users with an outline of the methods used and relevant statistics from the samples providing the data.

For the National Curriculum assessments standardization procedures will include teacher moderation, meaning that teachers' marks or classifications or ratings (which involve judgements, that is, subjectivity is introduced even though guidelines are supplied) will be open to amendment. The evidence for adjusting an individual teacher's assessments will be partly statistical (when level distributions appear abnormal) and partly based on consensus obtained from a group of peers. Though it is believed that generally the teacher's ratings will be the assessments likely to be changed, it may be possible for SAT marks or levels to be changed if the interpretation of marking guidelines could be modified.

Validity studies

In my view there is no doubt that test validation is the most neglected aspect of test construction. An analogy might be drawn with building construction, on the occasions when the designer and builder simply leave the inhabitants to live with the edifice.

A convenient way out, for test constructors, is to compare scores for a new test with scores from an established test. In other words, to design a correlational study of concurrent validity involving a sample of pupils taking several tests of the same or different attributes. Also other measures (of pupils) can be incorporated such as teachers' examination marks, observation ratings, pupils' self-ratings, health, attendance or social variables.

Studies which give inter-correlations with other tests of the same nominal attribute leave a question mark over the reason for developing a new test. But if the rationale claims that the new test measures an attribute differently (or better), then the appropriateness of correlating with another measure is raised.

In fact a properly designed study would include two or three different types of assessment made of the same attribute (multi-method) *and* the same range of methods applied to different attributes (multi-trait) (Campbell and Fiske, 1959). In this kind of design the hypothesis is that reliable measures of the same attribute will correlate more highly together than with similarly reliable measures of different attributes, whatever the method (thus demonstrating *concurrent validity*). When sub-scales are included, this approach can be very complex. However, the design ought ideally to include attributes which are supposed to be either uncorrelated or negatively correlated with the new test measure, again for a number of methods of assessment. The reason is that an attempt is made *to disprove* the hypothesis that the new attribute measure is independent of, or negatively related to, these other attributes.

Imagine, for example, that a new test of understanding mathematical concepts was correlated only with a previous mathematics attainment test score (for, say, 340 pupils attending eight primary schools). If the coefficient was 0.87, we could only conclude that the tests assessed the majority of pupils in much the same way. If a teacher's rating of 'problem-solving' and an observer's grade for 'practical investigations' were included, and the results were $r = 0.5$ (concepts with attainment test), $r = 0.7$ (concepts with problem-solving) and $r = 0.82$ (concepts with investigations), the validity of the new test would be fairly convincing. But if other measures of, say, pupil's age and teacher's rating for singing in tune correlated with an r of 0.7 and 0.8 respectively with 'mathematical concepts', we would have to think again.

There are statistical techniques for examining underlying factors inhering in multiple relationships, that is, multiple correlation and regression; factor analysis; and discriminant function analysis. For example, when the correlation patterns are further analysed into a number of factors, and when these factors line up with ones postulated in theories or derived from other, independent empirical studies, a test is said to have *construct validity*. On occasion the data will have to be collected up to several years after the new test is administered. This will have to be arranged and the follow-up exercise carried out.

Though it is extremely unlikely that one teacher's context will closely resemble another's, validity studies data should be supported with information which will allow a user to gauge whether or not his/her circumstances are similar or markedly different. If there are appreciable differences (for example, validity studies carried out with large numbers of pupils with samples chosen from schools, cf. one teaching group in a small school), the inference that validity will transfer across situations may be open to question. In any case, as was pointed out in Chapter 6, users ought to be prepared to carry out their own pilot study to learn more about the validity to a purpose of a test in their own context, as that is where its application is the most important.

Implications for teachers

Compared with 'test constructors', teachers are better placed to devise effective tests, when the assessments are sharply focused on the curriculum followed by their pupils. Perhaps the main point to be made is that time expended on devising sound assessments is an investment because the tests can be used in successive years, with fresh groups of pupils, provided that the objectives of the course planned for the pupils do not change much.

A prerequisite of devising test of pupils' learning is a well-planned course, which nevertheless can be modified according to the opportunities that occur from time to time. The course design will include a range of topics, activities, learning materials and tasks, projects, and so on, aimed at developing pupils' accomplishments. These might range from writing extensively on a theme to creating an original technical device, or for pupils experiencing learning difficulties the objectives might be closely targeted on to precise increments of learning.

In the assessment programmes outlined earlier in this chapter it was suggested that diagnostic evaluation should be the major focus between formal assessments. If this were done, all pupils would be involved, except for a small minority who have few difficulties. Hence, the pupils (and teachers) would become accustomed to examining errors or other difficulties, and, on occasions, using the 'chain back' principle (Ainscow and Tweddle, 1979) to find related aspects which a pupil could do confidently. This is nothing more than teaching for understanding, and the general aim of this should be to have pupils learn how to tackle their own learning problems, and become effective independent learners (Ainscow and Tweddle, 1988). For individual pupils, diagnosis might entail assessing attributes related to learning especially when the curriculum line of inquiry leads to an impasse. However, when learning has been well planned, the course objectives *and* learning tasks provide a ready-made set of assessment rationales.

The problem in moving from curriculum implementation to an assessment rationale is designing for a purpose. An unusual example is the assessment of primary pupils who have been tackling problem-solving and mathematical investigations working collaboratively. The purpose of the assessment was to discover the extent to which individual pupils were developing skills and insights. The context is such that the last type of test to be argued for is an essay. In fact, two approaches were proposed. In both cases children would investigate a problem without help from the teacher with pupils' activities decided by the group. One rationale argued for each group of pupils to mark their own project according to a scheme (discussing the problem, finding things out, trying different ways, presenting results) to give a project mark out of 30. They were then to decide each member of the group's share of the marks according to the work done. The second rationale made the case for interviewing the pupils as a group and then awarding each pupil two grades, one for conceptual understanding and the other for contribution to proposed solutions. Of course these assessments formed only part of the ones needed to cover all of the year's work; there were also periodic written examinations and a few multiple-choice tests of number operations.

A further aspect of assessing pupils is to provide a teacher with feedback on how well the course is going; what is successful in the course; and what needs to be revised or discarded. In this respect analysis of pupils' responses question by question, as for item analysis, is more useful than overall review of total scores. This technique would only be helpful when a test specification which reflects the curriculum is drawn up. (Without such a specification, the test or essay is not specifically sampling the field of learning promoted by the course.)

Item analysis, to give facility values, can be useful when collecting a pool of questions as a resource from which teachers can compile tests. The facility values give an indication of overall difficulty (the average of the facility values obtained from previous groups of pupils) relative to an age-group or ability band. For instance, one head of mathematics in a secondary school had organized questions under topic headings and had facility values, for sets of questions obtained from different year samples. In this way he could check over a period of time on such aspects as basic numeracy and decide whether to augment this component of course work for certain pupils. A significant advantage of his structured data-gathering and question storage/access system was that it saved teachers' time; tests could be compiled very rapidly and only a small number of new questions were needed periodically to keep abreast of changes in the curriculum. His information was stored on a set of file cards arranged in sub-sets by topics; but computer storage and retrieval would nowadays be quite feasible and a modest program would produce item data and estimates of test difficulty for varied selections of items chosen for particular groups of pupils.

Turning from test or examination questions to total scores, a factor which few schools take account of though widely acknowledged is the discrepancy between grade or mark distributions between subjects. When the marks are truly interpretable in terms of performance criteria, discrepancies between subjects would be irrelevant, in the measurement sense. But when marks have a notional basis in work which is 'average', 'exceptional', 'below average', and so on, discrepancies are likely to reflect markers' built-in models. Those who doubt this statement are invited to graph the distributions of grades or marks awarded by a number of teachers; a common finding is that the mean obtained lies above the 'average' (for example, more As and Bs than Ds and Es). Whilst there is no compelling case to be made for a normative base, there can be good reasons for examining the data and asking what assumptions and practices underlie its characteristics. (In one instance a teacher whose marks were always well above those of his colleagues said, 'If I teach them, they must be good'; unfortunately the external examiners rarely agreed.)

One school found that the discrepancy between subject mark levels led to difficulties when advising pupils and parents on the choice of optional subjects during the third secondary year. The problem was tackled by standardizing the score distributions for the year-group examinations, so that each one had the same mean of 50 and SD of 15. This was done on the school computer. No attempt was made to average the standardized marks as the purpose was to provide a common baseline for the appraisal of attainments. Contrary to expectations, the staff saw the benefits of the technique and the parents seemed to understand its explanation as a method for improving comparisons of performance.

One major aspect of test construction which teachers could adopt is the validation of their own testing or assessment procedures. The methods outlined in Chapter 6, to produce expectancy tables, when predictions have been made can be very illuminating, perhaps more so than correlations. One somewhat unorthodox though sensible use with older pupils is to show individuals how their earlier results relate to later ones; this information can initiate counselling discussions focused on academic progress.

The aspects discussed in this and the preceding technical chapters deal with the features which well-constructed tests should embody, as specified in the recommendations made by the British Psychological Society (BPS, 1980) and the American

Educational Research Association and its affiliated bodies (APA, 1985). Both sets of standards are intended to safeguard the public's interests and so stress ethical use (as discussed later in Chapter 9). The American publication also emphasizes purposeful use which should be valid in the sense that testing benefits those who have been tested.

Finally, it is not suggested that the assessments made by teachers should come to resemble stereotypes of 'tests'. To reiterate the point made at the beginning of this section, the rationale should justify how to reflect the variety of course contents and learning activities. These could include extended, prepared and amended pieces of writing, practical tests, 'live' performances and objective-type items, if and when appropriate. The assessments should match the pupils' educational experience. And the curriculum should be designed to fulfil educational ends as distinct from ends controlled by assessments.

CHAPTER 8
The Circumstances of Testing

In earlier chapters various conditions which might influence pupils' test performance have been mentioned and these are now considered more fully. The topic is important because the interpretation of results and any consequent decisions may be affected. Three aspects are considered: (1) situational effects; (2) individual factors; and (3) features in the test.

Situational effects

One of the properties of standardized tests is the uniformity of content and response options made available by the assessor. Test administration instructions are designed to ensure that the control over test content is not vitiated by undesirable effects. As far as possible, therefore, pupils taking a test are given the same verbal and written instructions, the same demonstrations and the same timings of test sections (when these apply). Other conditions, such as adequate seating and desk space, distance from other pupils and freedom from distractions, are regulated. Also the immediate environment should not present any clues which might prompt correct or incorrect answers (for example, wall charts, maps, Mathematics tables, flow diagrams, pictures).

Test instructions also stress that the invigilator's manner should be appropriate; in particular, that care should be taken to present the test in an encouraging yet businesslike way. At the same time, invigilators ensure that the pupils complete their personal details accurately and understand how to respond to the test items. These matters may seem pretty commonplace for hardened test takers, like teachers, but they can be a source of great distress to children with little experience of the situation. This point is seldom addressed in test manuals, though the selection tests given to 11-year-old pupils invariably have a 'practice test'. This is a short, usually easy test composed of the same item types as the main one which is attempted after the children have had a short break.

As the main aim of the testing procedure is to assess pupils with regard to an attribute, it makes sense to ensure that any obstacles which might obtrude should be removed. So when tests which are not familiar in format or response demand are to be given, those organizing the procedure should arrange for pupils to be given some preparatory experience. This applies particularly in primary schools because tests or examinations may be unknown to the children. For example, one primary head returned a set of trial English tests without giving them to the pupils, saying that they were not expected to stay in the same place for more than 20 minutes at any time during the day. Furthermore, as all the work was based on projects, attempting short answer test questions would be neither interesting nor productive for the pupils. These would be somewhat disadvantaged if their secondary school tested pupils shortly after their arrival without familiarizing them with the situation.

Some individually administered tests require a standard presentation of questions in an interview situation. In this setting the demands placed on the person giving the test are extensive. Teachers involved in these sessions have initially been inclined to teach the pupil they are working with; also they employ a repertoire of non-verbal cues to guide pupils towards an acceptable answer. The test manuals should indicate the recognized sequence of interactive prompts, if any are allowed. In such an event, the teacher/tester should rehearse administration routines and personal manner (possibly with video tape observation) before undertaking a serious assessment.

Good test administration requires familiarity with the materials and instructions for the pupils. When combined with a comfortable emotional atmosphere (often called 'rapport'), the situation can be helpful to the pupils. A point which test manuals tend to avoid, however, is whether the pupils should be given an explanation as to why they are doing a test. For some purposes, such as taking the next stage of a graded subject assessment, the reason is obvious. For others it seems only reasonable to explain as clearly as possible why a test is being given, provided that this does not prejudice the situation.

It follows that if pupils and teachers are to be enabled to prepare for a test, advanced planning and organization is needed. For some LEA exercises teachers nominated by the schools attend one-day seminars to be introduced to the test materials and to have a briefing on the conduct of sessions. One point which teachers make is that group sizes may have to be adjusted to take account of potentially disruptive individuals. Like many of the other activities undertaken by schools, commonsense and foresight, together with 'local knowledge', go a long way.

A further matter which should be considered is the effect on relationships between those doing the testing and those being tested. Assessment carries a range of social overtones; assessors are in a superior position, and usually their right to exercise judgement is accepted because the set-up of the system encourages the status quo. However, there is a need to question the judgement bases adopted by testers and other examiners, even when rationales are openly stated. As pupils cannot do this, it is up to teachers to take up points or major concerns. Of course when pupils feel that they are merely the objects of testing and that no benefits will come their way they might well become disruptive or quietly sabotage the part of the proceeding which they *do* control, that is, their responses. It follows that teachers ought to take social relationships into account when contemplating testing, in addition to during testing and the follow-up period.

These points apply to the standardized assessment tasks related to the National Curriculum targets, perhaps even more so regarding the last one pointing out the social implications. Teachers and pupils alike will find that parents will take a wide variety of roles, from demanding extensive rehearsal and explanation – with high expectations placed on children – to accepting the situation and supporting pupils without raising their anxieties. It will fall to headteachers mainly to attempt to foster this latter kind of relationship.

Individual factors

Whilst the situation may be regulated satisfactorily by anticipation and attention to detailed circumstances, the factors which may influence test performance among pupils are less amenable to control. Pupils may be well or poorly motivated because previous experience with tests may have been enjoyable or downright puzzling. Temperament can be extremely influential, to the extent that anxious pupils become inhibited, even to the extent of 'seizing up'.

In America 'test anxiety' is a recognized syndrome and has been researched extensively. Its operation can be indiscriminate, so that highly able and, in other circumstances, confident individuals are affected. It is probable that anxiety is increased when pupils realize that big decisions as well as social kudos hang on the results. It is generally thought that some anxiety acts as a spur, but it is likely that being anxious to do well is qualitatively different from worry over being tested.

The converse of anxiety is stability. Here again the immovably stable pupil might be unaffected by the testing situation and simply fail to exert any effort. Some tests might favour pupils who are at one pole or the other of the anxiety–stability dimension. For example, speeded tests in which quick reactions are evoked tend to favour the more stable pupils.

Other widely acknowledged personality factors: extroversion vs introversion, conscientiousness vs casualness, curiosity vs indifference and extrinsic vs intrinsic rewards, can affect performance. However, these may also interact with the situation presented by the test circumstances. For example, pupils who become keen on collecting certificates (extrinsic reward) might find the demands of speaking in a group oral test difficult to cope with if they are temperamentally introverted.

Whilst some of the variations commented on have been researched in relation to pupils making efforts at school studies (Sumner, 1976), there appears to be little by way of inquiry on their effects on test performance. A similar observation can be made about social class. Increasing numbers of studies have shown that measures of social and economic background correlate moderately well with progress and attainment in school, but there are no studies focused on test performance in relation to socio-economic factors.

A practical question is: 'what can be done about the variations attributable to these individual characteristics?' Unlike the score adjustments that can be made to compensate for age effects, the answer is 'very little', in the absence of definitive research confirming that satisfactory techniques can be devised and operated.

The catalogue of factors which may influence pupils' test performance might well be lengthy. In addition to those mentioned could be added: distractability vs concentration; attitudes towards the type of test material or the subject tested (in this respect positive or negative attitudes towards Mathematics relate quite highly to all-round attainments); the child's reading capability, especially range of vocabulary and level of abstraction; the child's graphical/spatial capabilities (and facility with other communication modes such as writing, speaking, listening, physical mobility and control, etc.); and the child's perceptual capabilities (visual, auditory and tactile acuity). In addition, there is a factor which is seldom mentioned, the child's liking for and response to the teacher administering the test (in my own experience there have been instances where a poor relationship has led a pupil to produce a deliberately bad result).

The foregoing remarks underline the provisional nature of test scores (indeed of examination grades or other types of assessment). Some pupils will be at their best on the day and others will never have a good experience during testing. Apart from regarding test scores as carefully derived approximations when decisions about pupils are being made, it is sensible to take account of knowledge about the pupil when considering each individual's result – which is not the same as saying that scores should be discounted or altered.

One way of encouraging pupils to focus attention and effort during testing is to offer feedback on the results. This can be done for individuals in counselling contexts and for groups as short written commentaries. For example, shortly after a series of assessment sessions started, an extremely disruptive pupil was promised an explanation of his results by a visiting assessor. The boy was regarded as 'sharp' but unreliable and a menace to all teachers. His results showed high verbal ability and English comprehension, high basic numeracy, high extroversion and anxiety, together with anti-school attitudes and extrinsically oriented motivation. He managed to check his initial uncooperative antics for the remainder of the sessions, then took an exceptionally keen interest in the tests and his results. Afterwards, it was reported that he seemed to be quieter and willing to employ his talents in schoolwork and drama. Of course the feedback in this case was non-technical and skilled, with the pupil being drawn in to discussion of implications and alternative points of view.

A further individual factor is the capability of the pupil to handle the language demands of tests. In some respects, multiple choice answer formats control the productive language variations between pupils, but the receptive side involved in comprehending the subject-matter of printed tests can have a large effect. An investigation of mathematics test questions presented in written form to one sub-sample of pupils and read over to another matched sub-sample showed that pupils who were above average on a reading test produced comparable levels of attainment. However, those pupils who were below average in reading and had to read the mathematics test themselves produced relatively poorer results. The implications of this finding are also supported by those obtained by the APU visiting assessors who administer tests verbally to individual pupils.

It follows that when a pupil is judged to have language capabilities which might limit test performance, when the object of the assessment is not language itself, the pupil should be given appropriate assistance. This may be problematic for attainment tests, but it presents no problems for questionnaires concerned with attitudes, personality or motivation. For young children, responses are often obtained by marking pictures (usually black and white line drawings); for these tests it is useful to keep an eye on children's reaction to pictures beforehand and to give those who may not be confident a rehearsal before the test is given.

The National Curriculum assessments, for the younger pupils especially, are intended to be similar to normal work situations in class. But inevitably, teachers in the role of assessors will have to employ certain controls on behaviour which may disort the assessments. Some pupils will not adjust readily to such conditions, especially when group tasks are employed; so the quality of the assessment may be prejudiced. It would be prudent for teachers to keep a note of any circumstances including a child's own behaviour which they consider may have affected a pupils' performance during a SAT session.

Test features

The last aspect, concerning language capability, brought out the interaction between the test, as a device, and the pupil, as an individual. The three aspects which impinge on the pupil are (1) the test administration, (2) its materials, and (3) responding to the questions.

Though usually test administration is straightforward, and invigilators should be alert so that any pupil with difficulties will be noticed and helped, there are some tests which have special conditions, such as time limits, which might affect pupils' performance. Other conditions, such as tape or video recording of oral or performance tasks, may place some pupils in uncomfortable situations unless time is allowed for rehearsal under relaxed conditions.

One feature of individually administered tests is the behaviour of the invigilator and his/her appearance or dress (young children have been intrigued by necklaces and ornaments on the hands and arms). One way of dealing with personal mannerisms (including speech) is to rehearse for a video recording, then to be recorded and the re-play reviewed by a colleague. Even simple matters such as glancing at a watch frequently come to notice and can be easily remedied.

For group invigilation points to watch are: adequate spacing of pupils; preparation of materials; clarity in giving spoken introduction and instructions; skilled use of apparatus (one French tape played only after several fumbling attempts killed off pupils' attention); a handy reserve of spare question books, answer sheets and other materials; the size of the group relative to the test task and supervision requirements; and the invigilator's attention is directed across the group not at any individual.

Test administration by computer also raises a number of issues. Briefly these are: whether or not the pupils tested are familiar with the situation, have keyboard facility and can use other equipment such as joystick, light-pen, etc.; the portion of printed instructions on the screen with repetition periodically as reference back (as in a booklet) is not possible; clarity of instructions and availability of help if needed; and that there is adequate practice opportunity, so that administration routines are familiarized.

The materials pupils see and handle in a test are important. For printed tests the paper should be opaque and good enough to be written on if responses are given on the test paper. Otherwise good-quality booklets are needed for repeated use. Likewise machine-scored answer sheets have to be of high quality and laid out such that pupils get a periodic check that they haven't skipped an answer or gone on to a wrong section. When the print is small, or in pink or pale blue, pupils should be asked whether they can read it satisfactorily.

A fairly recent innovation in testing is the use of 'answer-until-correct' sheets. Some types utilize a secret ink which is developed with a special pen to bring up a tick or a cross, others employ a latex film which is removed with a lollipop stick. These test answer sheets may need checking to ensure that the ticks and crosses do not 'show through' and so prejudice pupils' answers.

Whilst pupils' reactions to a test may be conditioned by its administration and materials, another factor which can affect performance is the response procedure. Multiple-choice answer sheets on occasion prompt theories such as 'only the middle three of five options contain the right answers' (not true, if the constructor has randomized them). Other frivolous attempts to work the system crop up such as marking each option in turn through the test. Hence all machine-readable sheets need careful scanning for indications of invalid responses, which should be extracted from the batch.

When a range of attributes is assessed through giving pupils a set of integrated tasks (as in some National Curriculum standard assessment tasks), the assessor has to cover a repertoire of responses and classify them according to specific rules. Systematic misinterpretation of any rule could lead to an error in assessment, as could a failure to observe a response accurately. In practice, because the teacher is involved in making subjective judgements across a variegated repertoire, the reliability of the results may be only moderate generally. Of course, some teachers will function consistently and accurately, others less so. But variations are found amongst any body of examiners (though they are seldom reported on) even though moderation procedures may have narrowed the initial range.

Test bias

Features which may also affect test performance, but which are less obvious, are bias in respect of gender, ethnicity or socio-economic background. In the USA test constructors are very aware that their products are subject to scrutiny and liable to challenge in the courts. Various attempts at producing unbiased tests have been made, called 'culture free' and 'culture fair'. These have content which is considered to be universal across the Western cultures or neutral with regard to any specific culture. Both concepts have been challenged, however, and the development of tests suited to specific cultures has been advocated.

In the UK, there is legislation which bears on testing applications if these relate to access to opportunities. The problem has its roots, as far as school education is concerned, in the 11+ selection procedures. When these were based mainly on verbal reasoning tests and headteachers' recommendations, girls generally obtained higher scores than boys. Thus a rather higher proportion of girls would be drawn from the mixed population when a single cut-off score was used. Some LEAs took the view, with the benefit of legal counsel, that selecting equal proportions of boys and girls for entry into separate-sex secondary schools was acceptable.

The situation is extremely complex because selection for an

educational opportunity is really quite different to selection for an immediate award, such as a prize, because it entails prediction. Hence validation of the procedure should take place over the duration of the secondary phase (Sumner, 1986), whatever selection methods are used. Nevertheless, the selection assessments should be examined for bias. This can occur in the separate tests (Goldstein, 1985) or in the make-up of the test batteries.

In fact it is a fairly simple matter to check for bias relative to gender because boys and girls are readily identified as such. Test constructors can then review (1) the test rationale, (2) the specification, (3) domain definitions, and (4) test item content, for any overt indications of bias. At the try-out stages they can also examine item analysis figures – mainly the facility values – to see whether particular questions have attracted markedly different levels of correct answers. Should this happen, the effect on the attribute domain of removing these items from the test can be evaluated. If the reduced set of items then present a distorted version of the domain, the conclusion might well be that there are differential tendencies which have to be accepted.

In some curricular areas such as Mathematics and Science there may be little room for bias, whereas in others such as Social Studies there might be a great deal, especially when socio-cultural background is considered as well as gender. Teachers should be aware of the problems of potential bias for several reasons:

- Individual pupils' results might be affected adversely.
- Tests (and examinations) need to be scrutinized for bias and attention drawn to material which might be contentious.
- LEA procedures which could affect individuals or groups, depending on test results, should also be reviewed critically.
- When tests contain items over which there is concern, evidence of bias should be sought, as merely asserting that there is a possibility of bias is not enough.

Hopefully, authors of future test manuals will refer to the

stages in the development of the materials which paid attention to gender and social and cultural factors.

A further kind of bias is possible when pupils are tested or assessed as members of a group when there is interaction between the group members or with the assessor/invigilator. For example, children in a lively, confident small group engaged in an investigation would be less likely to perform as well if they were put into other groups with children who were uncertain or less capable in, say, the oral components of the tasks. For survey tests done with samples of pupils who are anonymous and whose results are not given to their parents, such cluster effects are of no consequence. But for any National Curriculum tests which take place inter-actively in groups the influence of belonging to a particular class or sub-group is likely to be of great concern to parents and to the children's teachers. The technical point here is that some element of the assessment (score, grade, level) made of the individual pupil also contains a contribution from the group who were assessed at the same time. An ugly way of putting this circumstance is that each individual's result is contaminated by the group effect. Whilst it would be possible to investigate the size of the distortion (by changing group membership and using equivalent tests), the National Curriculum tests could not be treated in this way for reasons of teaching time and expense.

CHAPTER 9
Using Tests Purposefully

In an earlier chapter it was argued that tests should be employed only when the case for testing was justified as the most suitable assessment means for fulfilling an educational purpose. The converse also applies; that is, if other kinds of assessment than tests are not most suitable, then a test should be used to take an educational purpose further effectively. In the case of the National Curriculum assessments of pupils, the combination of tests and teachers' assessments are to be used, though the tests will have the major function of providing yardsticks for teachers when moderating their own provisional assessments to give a final score or level. Implicit in this concept is the proposition that acting purposefully entails taking decisions which enable or support educational objectives. Whilst aims may be implied rather than formally stated, decisions involve the explicit use of information to apply criteria.

Designing for applications

The decision-making context and a related chain of events is illustrated in Table 9.1. The objective in this case is to decide which pupils, if any, should be assessed further by teachers with a view to 'Statementing' by a multi-professional team.

The application of tests in this way seems mechanistic to some teachers and a sensible use of technical methods to others. In fact the design does not exclude the sensitive use of

Table 9.1:　Learning difficulty identification

Procedure design	Commentary
School philosophy and aims ↓	General statement on the entitlement of individual pupils to curricula adapted to aptitudes, with special provision as necessary
Particular purpose ↓	To determine which of the pupils entering a given year-group should be assessed by specialist teachers
Specific objective ↓	To determine which pupils are in a low-attaining band, as indicated by norm-referenced standardized tests
Assessments ↓	Recently constructed tests with specifications which reflect contemporary Mathematics and English curricula; printed and oral modes
Data ↓	Each pupil in the year-group's standardized scores for age-group ($\bar{x}$ = 100, SD = 15) for two Mathematics and two English tests
Data treatment ↓	Classification of each pupil into one of three groups, using 90 as the cutting score: (a) all four scores below; (b) all four scores above; (c) mixed, some above and below
Decisions ↓	Pupils in group (a) will be assessed by specialist; parents will be informed; pupils in group (c) will be reviewed after six months
Evaluation of procedure	Teachers' six-monthly review of progress on all pupils will be related to the assessments; anomalies will be followed up

other kinds of information on children's circumstances, their physical state and relationships with other pupils as well as teachers. What it excludes is woolliness about criteria and the action which is to be followed.

If we are to consider how to evaluate the effectiveness of tests to achieve a purpose, we have to propose an alternative design for a procedure. In the case illustrated above a different specific objective would apply but the underlying purpose related to individuals in a low-attaining group still pertains. The hypothesis to be evaluated is that the same individuals are identified by the alternative procedures.

A comparison of two procedures could have one of two outcomes. These are: (1) both would identify exactly the same children; or (2) some different children could be identified. In the unlikely event of (1) the hypothesis can be accepted. When alternative methods are found to be equally effective, comparison of the methods rests on efficiency (time required, costs, availability of data, etc.) or other factors such as teachers' feelings about their involvement. Indeed when two methods are equally effective, efficiency is the crucial factor. For example, it might be shown that a review of records compiled in the previous year identified the same pupils and that the time taken by the teacher(s) concerned amounted to less than the time needed to set and mark the tests. Taking the additional benefits of lower cost and no loss of learning time into account the verdict would certainly go in favour of using records. Of course, if testing took less time and teachers thought there were other benefits (for example, potentially useful diagnostic information from the test data; an annual appraisal of standards relative to a fixed norm), it might be decided to continue with testing.

The more likely outcome is (2), that is, the two methods identify some different children for further assessment. In this event the hypothesis, that there is no difference in the composition of the identified group, *might* be rejected: it is a matter of degree. The appropriate test in this case is one which allows for the correlation between the results because the same children are involved both times. In such a case a critical ratio can be formed from the number of discrepant pupil classifications. Using the symbol $\bar{z}$ to indicate that the ratio has a normal distribution, its calculation is as follows:

$$\bar{z} = \frac{\text{difference between numbers of discrepant cases}}{\text{square root of sum of discrepant cases}}$$

With cells labelled as shown in the fourfold tabulation below, the formula is:

$$\bar{z} = \frac{b - c}{\sqrt{(b + c)}}$$

Say that in a year group of 80 children the criterion applied to test results gave 20 pupils in the low-attainers group, whilst the criterion applied to records gave 30 in the same category. The cross classification shows how many pupils were classified consistently by both methods and the number of discrepancies either way:

From review of records

From tests	Lower attainers	Higher attainers	
Higher attainers	17 (b)	43 (a)	60
Lower attainers	13 (d)	7 (c)	20
	30	50	80

The discrepant classification are those low on one and high on the other, or vice versa; altogether there are 24 of these, with 56 on which there is agreement. The formula for $\bar{z}$ gives:

$$\bar{z} = \frac{17 - 7}{\sqrt{(17 + 7)}} = \frac{10}{\sqrt{24}} = \frac{10}{4.898} = 2.04$$

Here the ratio is over 1.96 (the 5 per cent level of significance) but lower than 2.58 (the 1 per cent level of significance). Hence, the hypothesis that the difference between the results may be due to random factors can be rejected at the 5 per cent level of confidence (that is, there is a 1 in 20 probability that the difference could be a chance effect); in other words, the two methods are most probably not equivalent.

In this example the result leaves the verdict somewhat open. However, the test procedure had a middle category (c) of pupils who were borderline in some way. No doubt a similar category would be found from teachers' review of records. An obvious move, therefore, would be to examine how many of these pupils fell into the discrepant categories. Other relevant information might be included such as the backgrounds of pupils, costs incurred and lesson time. But the principal question really is: which is the most effective method? Hence other information would be required such as essay marks for the year-group and Mathematics grades. Using this data, the comparison of methods would be based on validity as judged by performance criteria.

Certainly the answer to the question posed by the comparison is not easy to arrive at, but the importance of the question cannot be dismissed. The justification for taking the question seriously is that, using tests, 17 pupils would be identified for further assessment and parental discussion, and these would be different from the seven other pupils identified from the review of records. It should be emphasized that the quality of *both* measures is important when validity judgements are made in this manner; an unreliable criterion assessment or one that fails to indicate accurately an authentic reflection of a domain cannot possibly show whether or not a test is sufficiently valid for the purpose in question.

Questions about efficiency and effectiveness should be raised whenever assessment alternatives are available. Furthermore, judgements should be based on data, and this can and should include the views of teachers engaged in trials.

A design like the one outlined here has to be projected before it can be implemented. A critical point in the projection is test selection or the choice of alternative assessments. Some valuable guidance can be obtained from books which review tests (Levy and Goldstein, 1984; Vincent *et al.*, 1983; Ridgway, 1987). These may be of limited utility, however, because test reviews apply to material which is inevitably becoming dated. They tend also to rely on scrutiny of the published materials rather than the experience of users who have administered the test and applied the results. The consequence is that the review lacks the benefit of authentic contexts and suffers from reviewers' gratuitous prejudices. For example, a norm-referenced reading test was said to be unable to tell teachers anything that they would not have known from working with the children. Let us say that the test in question gives the same rank orders to a class of children as teachers' ratings; in this event additional information is provided by way of standard age scores for individuals, and the derived group data. Whether the normed data has any practical uses is a debatable point, depending on context and purpose.

To push this point further it might be helpful to consider whether there is a distinction between instrumental (focused on decisions) and evaluative (focused on description) testing purposes. Imagine that a headteacher is asked by the school governors to report on reading standards in each of the year groups, then how might the head respond? One way would be to ask why the information has been requested, since the time and effort needs to be justified. The governors might say that in order to discharge their responsibilities (*The Education School Governing Bodies Regulations*, DES, 1981 and the Education Reform Act 1988) they need to know about standards. Pressed further, they might say that details of the reading schemes, whilst helpful, were insufficient to gauge the general level of attainment throughout the school, so that a description of performance is necessary. This argument, at first sight, presents the case for evaluation, that is, by reference to certain criteria, then what is the position? As a response to this situation, the head might administer a standardized test (for a year-group not involved in the National Curriculum Assessments), report the mean score and graph the distribution. However, an appreciation of the data might well imply that changes should be put in train; in this respect decisions are incipient.

Though the difference between obtaining data for instrumental and evaluative purposes is one of emphasis, in my view it is preferable to approach an appraisal with a design which is explicit, in that it says how the results might be applied. For example, the governors' request for information on standards could be met by designing an inquiry which could *potentially* lead to decisions about (i) grouping individual pupils, (ii) the use of teachers' and pupils' time, (iii) revision of the schemes, (iv) children's attendance at specialist reading centres, (v) collaboration with parents and (vi) fresh approaches to teaching immigrant pupils. This kind of scope would call for a set of specific objectives and a corresponding set of assessments, criteria and information handling methods. Much of the information required already is to hand in schools though it needs marshalling. And an approach which addresses operational details seems preferable to one which leaves conflicting opinions unresolved (for example, do the test scores show that standards are *good enough*?). The example given had its origins in parents' disquiet about the amount of project work done in a school where there was little formal reading teaching. The major question for decision, which at the outset was only implied, was whether to adopt new reading schemes for the lower age-groups.

Whether or not to test

It is neither feasible nor sensible to try to develop rules to answer this question. Even if there were good quality tests of relevance to every purpose schools might entertain, the answer might well be a qualified 'no' because other sources of information might be equally relevant and readily available. These sources include teachers' knowledge of individual pupils gained from classroom incidents or episodes and appraisal of work in train; progress through courses, especially those organized into phases or tiers; teachers' observations and levels allocated for profile components of National Curriculum key stages; pupils' own self-appraisals or ratings using a scheme developed by pupils and teachers; and records of achievement containing details of activities, awards, residential and work experience. Some of these assessments are idiosyncratic, but they concern highly valued experiences. Furthermore, the self-assessments engender something which external assessments cannot, that is, reflection based upon the pupil's own perceptions of learning and belief as to its value.

The other side of the question is whether a test is suited to the purpose envisaged. Ideally the purpose should be defined and a test designed accordingly. To a limited extent, this is possible when item banks are accessible. Large well-specified banks exist for LEA and school use: in Mathematics, English comprehension, verbal and non-verbal reasoning, advice on test compilation is available and the tests are printed to a high standard; for small quantities costs are high relative to those stocked in the usual way. For the most part, however, the users have to employ tests designed for unspecified situations and anticipated uses rather than for a particular application.

The National Curriculum tests (that is, the SATs) are designed to fulfil the four objectives identified in the TGAT report (see Chapter 1). However, as has been argued in Chapter 2 (and by others, for example, Murphy, 1988, and Qualter, 1988) the likelihood of a single test or assessment satisfying multiple purposes effectively reduces as the number of purposes goes up. Indeed, it seems probable that the summative and evaluative roles will draw on the test element heavily, whilst the formative and diagnostic roles will depend mainly on the teachers' assessments made between key stages, and possibly, other supplementary tests or assessments.

A more general model of teaching to reach specified goals, such as attainment targets might be useful in linking learning and assessment. Here the teacher's objective is to be effective, but ancillary purposes, such as providing information to students on their progress and for on-going records of achievement or the summative record of achievement could be served. For the situation illustrated in Figure 9.1, it is assumed that teaching has been planned according to a curriculum before the teacher meets the group of pupils to be taught.

Here the initial assessment is called *adaptive* because its purpose is to indicate to the teacher how to change the course

Figure 9.1: Teaching–learning–reporting paradigm

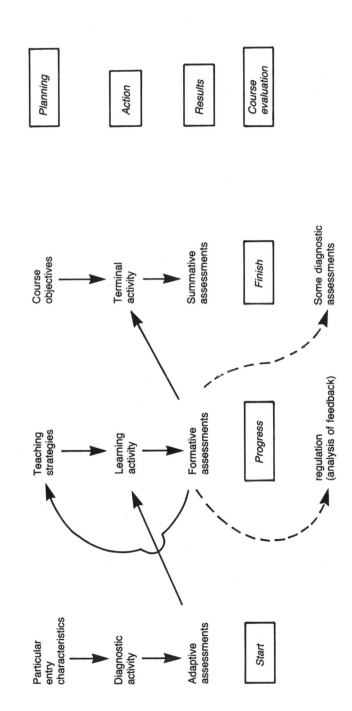

Planning

Action

Results

Course evaluation

Course objectives → Terminal activity → Summative assessments

Teaching strategies → Learning activity → Formative assessments

Particular entry characteristics → Diagnostic activity → Adaptive assessments

Start

Progress

Finish

Some diagnostic assessments

regulation (analysis of feedback)

work planned to make it accessible to the pupils (and this might also imply grouping the pupils for teaching on the basis of differentiated attributes). The *formative* assessments are principally to give pupils feedback on their attainments and provide the teacher with information about the quality of pupils' learning, the rate of progress and whether or not individuals are ready for the next stage or, possibly, if there is a need for further assessment focused on learning difficulties. This is usually called diagnostic, but there are two major aspects to this: one is a better, more detailed *description* of the problem, the other is designed to track down underlying related or prior features that can be hypothesized or *causal*. Clearly, the intensity and nature of the diagnostic assessment will affect the strategies planned and the classroom organization. Whatever the nature of the processes (class teaching, individual projects, graduated schemes, computer assisted, etc.), the final stages of a course should lead to an overall assessment concerned with the main course objectives. Though periodic assessments (sometimes erroneously called continuous) may have been used instead, it would be expected that the later ones should be designed to include some of the key material or attributes developed by the earlier work.

A final point is that the assessments could be tests or other forms of appraisal; but those used for causal diagnosis might well include a range of attributes, such as abilities or attitudes.

However, the question of whether or not to test is only worth asking if there are *seemingly* suitable tests which should be appraised when judging the aspects of its suitability. What follows is not a set of criteria for judging the validity of a test for a particular purpose. That can only be done by examining data obtained either from trials or very similar applications in contexts which match local circumstances. When appraising a test, it is helpful to consider the information given on the aspects listed below.

(1) *General information*	Title; Publisher; Date of publication; Date of related publications; When any previous versions were produced and country of origin; Price of booklets, answer sheets, manuals; Copyright; Author(s); Restrictions on use of results; Qualifications required of the user.
(2) *Applications*	Designated purpose(s) of tests; Population for whom appropriate; Score treatment relevant to proposed application with pupils; Test levels and variations in use of sections.
(3) *Attributes assessed*	Specified traits; Aptness of trait labels; Utility of traits assessed; Independence of separate traits claimed to be measured; Novel aspects of traits; Credibility based on research; Relevance of traits to any stated *testing purpose*.
(4) *Test format*	Presentation of print, diagrams, apparatus, booklet(s), answer sheets; Identification of parts, packaging; Convenience for use in school, clinic or elsewhere; Attractiveness.

(5) *Administration*

Materials;
Time allowance, if any;
Practice test;
Instructions, clarity and
  completeness;
Training advisable or required (by
  author/publisher or professional
  association or LEA/government);
Sequence of events;
Special requirements, e.g. stop-
  watch, slide projector, tape
  recorder, video, computer.

(6) *Scoring*

Scheme for marking;
Score key;
Record sheets or charts;
Conversions to other scales, e.g.
  norms, percentiles, 'log odds' or
  derivations;
Stencils, machine reading;
Guessing allowance;
Degree of objectivity/subjectivity
  in awarding scores;
Any complications;
Rate of scoring;
Costs of scoring;
Treatment of standard error of
  score.

(7) *Judgement basis*

Norm reference or proficiency
  (criterion referenced);
Type of norm, e.g. percentile,
  standardized score, grade bands,
  classifications;
Types of samples normed or
  appraised;
Quality of samples reported, i.e.
  representativeness, size, sex,
  social background;
Motivation of samples;

Drop out from target samples;
Aids to interpretation, e.g. graphs,
 tables, expectancy charts,
 profiles.

(8) *Test development*

Rationale specification;
Trials of items and analyses;
Facility and discrimination values;
Reliabilities, i.e. internal
 consistency, stability over time,
 equivalence between forms or
 versions;
Types of coefficient;
Correlations between test sections
 and sections with total score;
Effects of speed/time restrictions;
Standard error of score, its
 evaluation;
Significance of profile score
 differences;
Factor analyses or other construct
 validity investigations.

(9) *Validity*

In relation to purpose(s);
Methods used for establishing
 validity;
Types, i.e. predictive, concurrent,
 conceptual content, construct,
 face;
Quality of data, e.g. significance
 level of correlations;
Any indications of bias in data
 interpretation;
Sample sizes and nature of samples;
Cross validation of profiles or
 prediction equations (i.e.
 application of coefficients
 obtained from one set of trials
 with another, independent
 sample in a later trial).

(10) *Test manual*
Completeness, re above headings;
Technical level, clarity of layout
    and writing;
Persuasive or emotive terminology;
Academic quality, i.e. rigour,
    reference to theory and allied
    work;
Candour on shortcomings;
Durability.

In such an appraisal the test manual is just as important as the test itself. It should be read critically; test authors and publishers incline towards unqualified optimism when claiming what a test measures and asserting its usefulness.

The importance of reading tabulated data cannot be over-emphasized. Tables are compiled from the responses of samples of pupils and the resultant scores. For example, one widely used test of reading is said by the author to be suitable for pupils from 6 years 5 months to 12 years 10 months, though from age eight years upwards the caveat is given that the test is mainly suited to below-average pupils. In fact the standardization tables show that 'ceiling effects' are apparent with the better pupils for 'normal' samples of seven- to eight-year-olds (i.e. about 50 per cent of the pupils obtain maximum scores); for older age-groups the effect is even more marked.

The test user is in something of a bind on the matter of validity for a specific purpose. Careful appraisal along the lines shown above should at least avoid a disastrous choice of test. But the only firm basis for judging suitability is use in context. For this reason, if there is to be large-scale use, it is worthwhile setting up a trial situation.

After a trial or genuine application a number of questions can form the basis for a review. These are set out below, in the left-hand column, whilst procedures for furnishing answers are given on the right:

Review question	*Procedure*
Was the test age range suitable for your group of pupils?	Examine raw score distribution for 'floor' or 'ceiling' effects if test is normed (i.e. large numbers of children awarded very low, or very high, scores).
How did the children cope with test items?	Carry out a simple item analysis for the whole group or a random sample of about 400 pupils' scripts. Ask a sample of pupils.
Were the contents/tasks suitable?	Conduct an item-by-item classification; compare with curricular guidelines or other basis (theory, experienced teachers, panel views).
What factors might have affected pupils' performance?	Review test administration reports for difficulties (materials, time, interruptions, language, instructions).
Was the test biased?	Examine score distributions for boys/girls and ethnic minorities.
Did results broadly confirm expectations?	If appropriate, correlate test results with other data (teacher's records/grades, comparable tests/pupils' self-ratings).
Were the results consistent?	Examine the effects of standard error of score determined confidence bands when decisions are based on maximum and minimum scores respectively: how many pupils would be treated differently?

| Was the application valid for the purpose defined? | Check results against current evidence or later information (teachers' opinions, grades, ratings, examinations, training course results, etc.). |
| How did the pupils respond to the test and comment on it afterwards? | Sound out reactions informally or use an evaluation questionnaire. |

It is clear from the earlier chapters, and the preceding sections of this one, that testing should not be approached lightly. The most critical aspect is the definition of information needs in relation to decisions whether specified or implied. Consequent questions relate to whether or not a sound design can be devised; whether the data handling and interpretation skills are available; and whether suitable tests (and other means for gathering data) can be obtained.

The issues are complex. On the one hand, schools may seek advice (from other schools, the psychological services, colleges or universities and research organizations and publishers), and on the other hand, they can explore problems (and designs and tests) first hand, to develop pragmatic methods based on the use of data and its systematic evaluation. Trials of this kind do not have to involve huge numbers of pupils and, though the analysis of the item and test data may be intensive, the work can be interesting in its own right, partly because of its close involvement with pupils who are known. So whilst other people's views and expertise can be extremely helpful, they cannot provide the insights that can be gained in the environment of a particular school (so-called 'ecological validity').

Testing is only part of teachers' and schools' means and ends. Used judiciously, tests fit the warp and weft of teaching and assessment. Chapter 10 considers testing in the wider educational fabric.

CHAPTER 10
Perspectives on Testing

Contexts

The literature on evaluation abounds with arguments for and against testing pupils. On the one hand, how pupils measure up against performance standards or compare with others is an imperative; on the other hand, contexts and processes are paramount. In parallel with these viewpoints are contrasting types of evaluation, sometimes called 'the agricultural model' and 'the anthropological model', measuring variables related to conditions as compared with observing cultural systems. Other terms might be used such as 'hard-nosed' vs 'naturalistic' and 'product' vs 'process'. These misleading typologies exaggerate the prejudices of their protagonists. Process evaluators are accused of avoiding the crunch issues concerned with what pupils have learned and are competent to do by the end of each phase; product evaluators are derided for failing to understand the educative experiences and believing that it can be encapsulated in lists of arid target criteria.

Teachers might ask, how do wrangles about methodology affect them. But they have only to consider the calls for accountability and higher standards, coupled with systemic changes in governors' responsibilities, LEAs interventionist activities and central government's schemes, to realize that evaluation in its many guises is already part and parcel of professional life. The language speaks of monitoring, appraising, assessing and recording, and the main focus is pupils' curricular progress, followed by schools, then LEAs. Indeed these targets are very limited compared with the scope defined when the objectives of comprehensive education were formulated for study in the late 1960s (Ross *et al.*, 1972).

Also the language is managerial not only for heads, but for all kinds of teachers. So management objectives and management information, and the associated logic of knowing where one is in order to move towards the next objective, come to the fore. In parts of the USA there are statewide 'assessment programs', with compendia of objectives and batteries of grade-level criterion-referenced tests. In the UK there are increasing numbers of 'graduated' tests and assessment in a prolific array of structures, procedures and impressive certificate headings. Then, from 1992 on, there are the target-based tests or assessments of attainments in the National Curriculum 'subjects'. Where does this leave the teacher? As Hargreaves (1986) has indicated, one can dream that sensitive teaching which values all individuals and their talents will be encouraged through these extensive assessment systems; or the vision can turn into a nightmare where certificate gathering (or level climbing) becomes the dominant culture and education is debased.

In some respects, the UK is highly vulnerable to the extension of examinations and other formalized assessments into every phase and stage of education because we have had (and continue with) a system which regards accredited success as essential. Its attractions and main value lie in its currency, provided that the trading partners have something to offer in return. For younger children few would doubt that the payoffs from 'doing well' in tests or other assessments should be minimized. Nevertheless, a seemingly compelling case can be put for assessing each pupil at various points in their school careers, to evaluate progress relative to peers, to self, to learning objectives and to attitudes towards school and education (though the latter was excluded by the TGAT).

As an instance of the kind of process which might result, one American text on measurement and evaluation lays out a model programme of assessments. The majority of the assessments take the form of commercially published objective-type test batteries, most with multiple-choice machine-scored answer sheets. For young children in kindergarten there are 'readiness tests', for the other age-groups the tests are mainly norm-referenced 'achievement' series, including Mathematics, English, Science, Social Studies and History; some ability tests are included. Over the six to 16 age range a pupil would be given 84 separate tests, some organized into batteries. A large number of these have sub-tests and computer printouts which show the results as profiles or are keyed against defined objectives. Some of these, in turn, are referenced to particular textbook pages where content related to test topics will be found. This type of information is presented as diagnostic as well as showing aspects of progress in a clear manner. Additionally, some of the test results could be used to justify inclusion in federal or state schemes to provide additional resources for children with special needs. In a programme of this kind children would, of course, still have other types of tests or assessments related to class or home work and various kinds of course-based assessments. At the time of writing the National Curriculum 'subject' profiles and attainment targets for the ten assessment bands are not finally laid down. But it is clear that the core of three subjects will have at least eight components; and if the remaining seven foundation subjects are treated similarly, there will be 20–30 formal assessments made of pupils at the age of 11 and 14 years.

There is no objection in my view to an extensive test programme of the kinds alluded to, provided that a purposeful use of the information is defined at the outset, and it is imperative that the diversity of educational attainments which are not reflected by the test results are recognized and valued. These attainments would include using spoken and written language to express emotions, convey facts, transact business, explore ideas, describe activities, organize material and engage in learning in many disciplines. Innumerable parallels can be given for various other disciplines; for example, music teachers using electronic keyboards not only aspire to have all pupils play the instrument and read notation, they want them to compose, so performance and composition would be assessed (indeed, as the GCSE provides for).

The foregoing discussion underlines aspects of evaluating pupils' attainments which could well be taken as principles. These are that (1) assessment aims should be distinguished from education aims, though the latter may encompass the

Figure 10.1: Contribution of objective-type testing relative to education evaluation

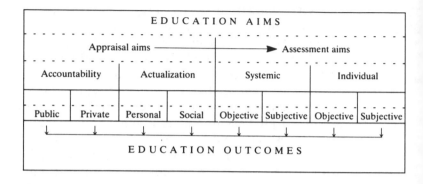

former, (2) assessments for systemic purposes should be distinguished from those intended for individual learning purposes and (3) objective-type standardized tests should be distinguished from subjective-type interactive assessments. Though these distinctions may not be clear-cut, they provide a framework for placing tests in the contexts of appraisal and assessment, as suggested in Figure 10.1.

The diagram reminds us that people are concerned collectively and personally about their satisfaction with provision and the outcomes of education, to which the ethical response is accountability. It also indicates (see, for example, Vallance, 1986) that personal and social goals can be realized through the development of attributes in society and in individuals (that is, recognizing one's talents and pursuing their development, 'self-actualization' in Maslow's, 1954, terms). A major point, however, is that objective-type tests (of attainment, attitude, proficiency, motivation, ability, personality, circumstance, learning style, etc.) comprise only a minor part of the information supply which the evaluation of education requires. The 1988 Act and TGAT assessment scheme of attainment targets ranged over ten levels embodies some aspects of the features outlined above. For example, public reports of a school's or a class's results is linked to accountability; formative interpretation can only apply to individuals, as can the further diagnostic assessment to keep track of pupils whose progress causes concern. And using the results to group pupils for teaching by level rather than age would be a systemic application. But it is limited by its managerial imperatives, which fail to capture the ideal of self-actualization; the schools and teachers (using the broader records of achievement) may aspire to do that.

Test developers seek to extend the scope of their products. In many ways they are right to do so, for when other forms of assessment come under the miscroscope, they are found to lack accuracy and to defy interpretation. This is particularly so when it is assumed that the test milieu *must* apply to all forms of assessment. Hence the territory for the debate is that already staked out by the testers. The factors of reliability and validity are raised for scrutiny; for example, what are the correlations between individual essay markers or dance adjudicators: do they agree on the qualities they take into account when awarding a particular mark? Assessments by other methods, such as observation of pupils during class, usually show that there are shortcomings, compared with carefully trialled and developed tests. To some extent, these are important questions but they are adjuncts to good practice, not its kernel.

Apart from querying whether a mark or grade or level is necessary or even helpful, the central issue is aptness (fitness for purpose) and validity *in context*. A good example comes from a small group of teachers who aimed to assess what children learned from project visits. Hitherto they had expected children to write three or four paragraphs with the help of notes made during the visit. This account would usually have a drawing to accompany the narrative or other illustration such as a photograph or visit brochure. By and large, the teachers felt that this written assessment failed to reflect the curiosity displayed by the children and the diverse kinds of learning the experience afforded. After reviewing what the children saw and did, who they listened to and talked with, and the materials they handled and collected, the group decided to assess the visit through structured interviews. These revealed a range of understandings which surprised the teachers for their content and maturity and also indicated how much better use could be made of any follow-up written work.

The discussion so far may seem sceptical of testing. However, it has not recognized fully the distinction between standardized norm and proficiency (criterion-referenced) tests and tests constructed by teachers which are related closely to the coursework planned for the pupils. Nor has it taken into account the generally inappropriate, stereotyped assessments which are commonplace in many schools (Engel-Clough, Davies and Sumner, 1984) which, hopefully, the National Curriculum assessments will replace. Briefly, in this study focused upon early secondary-age pupils, it was found that most of the formal assessment consisted of written examinations, which followed the style of external 16+ examination papers. Schools were found which even graded the homework done by 12-year-olds as if it was an external examination submission (and parents were given a guide to the system). Procedures of this kind could hardly inform a child's understanding either of the assessment itself or, more demandingly, of the area of the curriculum being studied.

At the secondary stage, the GCSE examination with its component of direct teacher assessment has encouraged the demise of such negative practices. Despite the permutations of course components into combinations intended to relate pupils' demonstrated capabilities to successive grade levels, pupils should benefit from the emphasis placed on matching assessments with course components. They should also benefit from the acceptance of teachers' structured observations as an appropriate method of assessment for accreditation.

Of course accreditation has a different purpose from the various graded assessments currently emerging. These aim to mark progress in successive steps and also to encourage pupils by recognizing achievement. Overall the secondary schools face an array of external assessments on a scale which has not previously been seen. And these can increasingly involve pupils' own contributions from the age of 11. Indeed this form of self-based (sometimes termed 'ipsative') assessment is coming to be accepted as important in its own right, possibly because it underpins self-actualization.

Amidst this welter of assessment, including the periodic SATs, is there a place for 'standardized' testing? The answer depends on the delivery of benefits to the pupils in the form of published instruments. Both schools and authorities have to decide what these could be. A cardinal point, which has been stressed throughout this book, is that decisions should follow from the test result. A corollary is that implementation of decisions requires *adaptation* (by the teacher, the school or the system) and resourcing.

These factors can be illustrated by referring to one authority's procedure for enhancing children's early language learning, especially in reading. A team of support teachers has been recruited to work on the basis of one teacher to eight infant classes over four days in the week. The support teachers spend the remaining day at the learning resources centre, on materials development and feedback. The team teacher arranges with each class teacher how the work should be organized, one dealing with children making steady progress and the other attending to the lower-attaining group. Initially, these are identified by how they respond to a standardized assessment, developed at the centre. This involves listening and reading, with the material chosen to represent everyday experience common to all children (life in 'our road') in the local, urban environment. The assessment is administered to the children in their classes: conditions are as for testing; the assessments are marked but not scored; the outcome is a classification into one of two groups within the class on criteria which apply across the authority; and some account is taken of children's circumstances (ethnic origins, working mother, single parent, siblings). The process is evolving, that is, still adapting, and is moving on to include early learning in Mathematics.

Under the current provision of education there are a number of turning-points in pupils' school careers at which careful appraisal is essential, for individuals and groups. These are on transfer between stages for younger children and when choosing 'options' for older pupils. Between these points there are a great many facets of development, some of which can be regarded as of major significance; for example, intellectual satisfaction gained from independent study and successful completion of design or problem-solving tasks; or gaining knowledge of personal attributes in relation to the demands of working.

Given that tests or other forms of standardized assessments

are to be administered to pupils at the end of the 'key stages', what might be a minimal programme for a pupil (in the UK) passing through the school system? Figure 10.2 suggests how the National Curriculum assessments might well be interspersed with others to aid in guidance and decision-taking.

Teachers might object to the amount of time being given to testing or assessing in addition to that required for the nationally prescribed ones. In fact, the group tests are extremely economical of time and administrative effort.

Parts of a programme of the kinds shown in the figure could well be supported by the LEA, especially those parts which impinge upon procedures which affect neighbouring schools. Transfer from primary to secondary, where test results can complement the official record, will utilize the National Assessment results, which form part of a pupil's school record. Schools enrolling an 11-year-old intake will need procedures to collate and analyse the data for the whole of this cohort and should also ensure that each teacher has the information in each pupil's performance to study closely *before* meeting the pupils he or she will teach for the first time. Of course an LEA could have policies related to the system (for example, staffing for special needs) which depend on test results, and these would be additional to the ones indicated.

It is clear from the figure that a testing programme of this nature makes certain demands on teaching time. To some extent, it is related to the core curriculum and so supplements teachers' own assessments. Indeed the largest amount of testing would be that forming part of teachers' assessments based upon coursework. Towards the later secondary years these would also contribute to the externally accredited assessments.

So far in the discussion the presence of external examinations has been accepted as one of the givens in the educational environment. Whether or not these serve a useful purpose is questionable in an era when progressively fewer pupils will enter employment directly from school at 16 (Secondary Headteachers' Association proposals, 1986). Without the external examinations, tests might be used more widely as vehicles for appreciating more thoroughly the attitudes, personal attributes and learning styles of individuals; these

Figure 10.2:   Outline for a minimal testing programme in the UK context

		Compulsory	*Optional*
Primary Stage	Infant 4–7 years	National Curriculum Tests across core of English, Mathematics, Science and Foundation subjects: age 6–7 years	Group test of initial progress in language and Mathematics: ages 5–6 years. ↓
	Junior 7–11 or 12 years	National Curriculum Tests, Core and Foundation: age 10–11 years	Individual diagnostic tests focused on learning difficulties, if any. Group reading tests, age 8 years. Group mathematics tests, age 9 years. Group non-verbal reasoning test, age 9–10 years. ↓
Secondary Stage	11 or 12 to 14 years	National Curriculum Tests, Core and Foundation: age 13–14 years	Individual tests aimed at diagnosing learning difficulties, if any. Group test for guidance, e.g. clerical, scientific, symbolic, spatial, mechanical reasoning: age 13–14 years. ↓
	14–16 years	External exams or National Curriculum tests, age 15–16 years	Careers related questionnaires ↓ proficiency assessments: age 16 years.
Tertiary Stage	16–17 or 18 years		Aptitude tests across a broad range ↓ Proficiency assessments.

purposes would relate to counselling and guidance, in which decision-taking resides with the individual.

However, whilst one of the aims of education is, or should be, to assist pupils to develop autonomy as learners, the practicalities of teachers' work casts decision-making as part of their role. When pupils are concerned (as they mostly are), there are extraordinary ethical responsibilities which involve not only caring relationships and intellectual integrity, but the teaching of ethics, whatever these are. In the field of testing a great deal is taken on trust, by pupils and parents, and by users such as teachers, education officers, advisers and psychologists, together with those offering guidance and pastoral care.

As the ethical use of tests is part of teachers' wider professionalism, the points which follow need not be laboured. They are divided into two lists: those which refer to teachers in relation to tests, and those which deal with the results obtained from testing:

Teachers and tests
- Choice of tests: the most appropriate for a purpose should be used; advice should be obtained if necessary.
- Security: stocks of tests should be kept in locked stores and issued only for approved use.
- Training: teachers should use only tests for which they have been trained (if training is required) or formally qualified (when required by the publisher/author).
- Administration: the methods specified by the author (or the government's assessment agency or an examining body) should be adhered to; should modifications be necessary, they should be in the spirit of the instructions, otherwise testing should be abandoned.
- Restrictions: any limitations specified by the publisher/author should be observed.
- Quality: ill-conceived or poorly constructed or inadequately scaled tests should not be used, even when they seem to be ideal for a purpose.
- Reporting: results should be given accurately in technical terms; they can be recast into other formats (such as graphs or charts) and contexts, such as results from pre-

vious years or other areas can be shown, with due reference to school factors or other contexts.

- Interpretation: when results are published appropriate interpretations can be given, for example, score, grade or level distributions can be linked with attainment criteria or diagnostic implications; when this is done there should be a basis (for reference) such as the assessment rationale, domain assessed, historical data, evidence from investigations, performance indicators of pupils' progress, etc.

Individual results

- Confidentiality: pupils' results should be given to those who 'need to know' with restrictions on communication made explicit. (Note: the requirements of the Data Protection Act relate to electronically stored or produced data and rights of access to it.)
- Security: score lists and other data about individuals should be kept in locked storage cabinets or rooms; codes which identify pupils should also be secure.
- Interpretation: scores should be related to a 'confidence band' or related score bracket; when others are involved this concept should be explained or incorporated in the score chart or recording system.
- Application: use should include appropriate design and use of technical methods.
- Verification: outcomes based on test results should be followed up.
- Context: relevant additional data should be taken into account, provided that it is reliable.
- Labelling: pupils should not be type-cast in such a way as to write off any positive expectations; whatever the results of a test, *all pupils can learn*.
- Recording: test results should be accompanied by details which identify the test and the date of testing.
- Feedback: whenever possible, feedback should be given to the pupil and others who ought to be involved including parents.
- Reports: only test data relevant to circumstances under consideration should be transmitted.

Finally, it is axiomatic that test results or the experience of being tested should not be detrimental to the interests of any groups or the individual pupil. Most of these points apply to governors, who will have access to all of the National Curriculum test results (for groups of pupils, not individuals).

Future developments

The attainment testing model (for the National Curriculum) of profile components containing attainment targets graded over ten successive levels seem likely to dominate the UK scene during the 1990s. The attempts to mirror the curriculum and classroom learning conditions with criterion-referenced multi-attribute tasks (integrated assessments) will have been evaluated; hopefully, the technical factors, rather than the political, will have led to more precise methods based on clearly defined domains. Meanwhile, away from attainment testing, computer networks will be extended to provide flexible access to assessments tailored to group situations or individual needs.

Recent trends in test development point to more sophistication. We can expect to see greater use of automated methods and intensive computer analysis of responses in order to exploit more thoroughly the information obtained. In some respects automation will share the same features as automation in other fields including de-skilling the human input; uniformity of production; limitless capacity for work; precision within machine parameters; adaptability to certain conditions; high operating speed; and access to complex interdependent processes.

At the time of writing, automated (or as some prefer to call it 'computer-aided') testing has been done mainly with existing standardized printed tests. As Bartram (1985) pointed out, this represents only a modest step into the arena. Of the five areas of testing (choice of instrument, administration, presentation of questions and responding, scoring and interpretation) the most accessible are administration, responding and scoring. The most problematic areas are choice of instrument and interpretation. These are the ones which will require 'expert systems' to be effective. In essence, such systems embody the knowledge and skills of a body of experts in a field, then make it accessible to others through the computer via sub-systems of interactive programs.

All this is a long way on from the computerization of existing tests. Even so, this development can raise problems (*Bulletin of the British Psychological Society*, December 1984) because there may be effects due to administering items one by one on a visual display screen and obtaining responses on a keyboard. Unless these 'vehicle' effects have been investigated, any reliance placed on score interpretations from printed version norms has to be regarded as misplaced. It follows that when well-known and widely accepted tests are computerized, those responsible should carry out studies on the equivalence of performance. When differences are found, or in the absence of any evidence of equivalence, norms for the computer version of a test should be established independently. A further issue is that similar score distributions for printed and computerized versions is insufficient evidence for equivalence because the same individuals tested with both versions might obtain significantly different scores. Hence high inter-version correlations are needed before printed version norms can be used for computer version results. Anyone using a computerized version of a test should be aware of these requirements; similarly, anyone publishing such a version should carry out the studies and publish details in a manual supplement.

In the near future teachers can expect to see both purpose-made computer-administered tests and computerized versions of printed tests. Whilst there are many unique advantages in using computers, there is a danger that the technology will acquire its own authority but at the same time, removing it from the understanding of many users. The safeguard lies in the hands of users, who should study the evidence on validity in relation to purpose(s). If none is published, they should not use the test on ethical grounds; they should also write or use electronic mail to request details of validated applications.

Even at this time, some of the advantages of computer-based tests can be described. These include:

- the generation of items from stored data and structural

rules – for some domains this facility could provide an infinite number of items;
- access to complex item forms based on multiple classifications within domains or on multi-facet theories;
- tests 'tailored' to suit individuals, based on their responses to previous items;
- data on timings of interactions between test question elements and individuals;
- virtually instantaneous scoring and scaling for display, printout or data transmission;
- high-speed routines for examining profile match, regression equation predictions or expectancy table probabilities;
- facilities for rapidly 'adding in' additional information from tests and other sources on social and personal characteristics;
- access to extensive stores of interpretation data, especially for diagnostic purposes and comparing with characteristic data-based models.

These are exciting possibilities which would well be paralleled by advances in learning methods and in other modes of assessment; there are dangers, in that the technology could be both persuasive and obscure. However, the user has the final say provided that the *fundamental test of a test* is not neglected, that is, the results are examined for validity in respect of a defined purpose in a specific context.

Conclusions

In the latter stages of drafting this material, I asked several teachers and colleagues the question: 'what are the substantive issues in testing?' Answers were varied and included aspects such as:

- ensuring that tests are of good quality, conceptually and technically;
- achieving clear benefit to the pupils;
- changing from norm referencing to criterion referencing;

- training teachers in testing procedures, especially standardized administration;
- making a better range of tests available, especially ones that will aid the identification of learning problems;
- illustrating applications in the manuals whilst putting technical data into appendices;
- giving users better information for judging between tests – at present test choice depends too much on hunch;
- providing teachers with modern technology aids to testing, especially data processing and score interpretation.

Each person had an individual emphasis; there is no accepted list of issues. I have included those which have emerged as important from experience as a teacher using tests and as a test constructor; these are recapitulated in the following summary.

The principal theme of this book is that tests have an important place in the range of assessments used by teachers. On occasion tests provide unique data which other forms of assessment are not designed to yield. Importantly, tests may be the most efficient and fair means of assessment of several available methods. These conditions may not always prevail, so teachers and other users will need to be alert to the issues and be prepared to obtain data from trials in order to base evaluations of particular approaches on evidence rather than assertion.

Using tests properly demands a certain understanding about their basis in theory or the curriculum and rationales which connect these with pupils' circumstances and teachers' purposes. A critical point is the variable nature of measurement, arising from the necessity to draw samples, of questions and responses, of pupils and of occasions. Hence measures from tests should represent justified approximations within confidence bands. Raw score transformations to other scales are used, but these should contribute to the interpretation of pupils' performance, as expressed in the recorded results.

A principle, which has been stressed throughout the text, is that tests should be used to enable educational purposes to be realized effectively. Doing so requires a willingness to examine test data, by the use of technical methods, and at all times by reference to the context of an application. Purposiveness, it is argued, is ensured by planning designs for obtaining and applying test results which lead to decisions which, in turn, enable the realization of educational objectives.

Care in choosing and using tests is essential. Hence judgements of test quality and appositeness are needed. These can only be made when test manuals are read critically and other sources of information consulted. However, as information from these quarters may be partial or biased, it may be helpful to plan and carry out trials. Certainly, when there might be problems in the immediate context (pupils' ethnic origins, teachers' attitudes, pupils' capabilities in relation to test features, match with curriculum, and so on), trials are essential.

Tests in the immediate future and long term are likely to become more complex, though administration and interpretation may be de-skilled when procedures are automated. Similarly, interpretation of pupils' results may be handled by computer. However, current ethical and practical imperatives still will, or ought, to pertain, in that decisions arising from tests should benefit pupils, hence validity in specific contexts should be demonstrated.

In common with other areas of education, in which there is conjunction of intention, theory and method, testing has complex features. However, when used caringly, test results can inform, but not supplant, the professional judgements of teachers.

Postscript

Moderation of assessments

Whereas objective-type tests prescribe answers as well as questions, other kinds of tests and assessments require the assessor (or examiner) to make judgements about pupils' responses or pieces of work. Assessors thus become a part of the measurement instrument, one that is potentially highly variable. They may differ, for quite understandable reasons. The following two examples illustrate several points.

(1) *Criterion-referenced statements*
   (a) The pupil can identify wood, metal and plastic.
   (b) The pupil can do a handstand.
   (c) The pupil has set up simple experiments using laboratory apparatus.

(2) *Gradings*
   (d) Letters A to E are to be awarded for essays that exhibit in greater or lesser degree construction, a narrative theme, clear expression, imagination, good syntax and spelling.
   (e) Marks on a scale of 0 to 100 will be awarded for an instrumental or vocal performance taking account of technical proficiency and expression: average performance should be given between 60 and 70 per cent.

In the first of these instances, (a) and (b) are 'can do' statements and (c) is a 'record of achievement' statement. Though each purports to deal with basic attainments, all of the criteria are open to interpretation. Cases (d) and (e) illustrate how assumptions about adjudicator qualities enter the measurement process. Extended assessments, of complex performances and coursework, incorporate aggregates of these interpreted measures.

To mitigate the effects of idiosyncratic or genuine variations between assessors, a range of procedures have evolved. These are usually referred to as 'moderation'. Though the term seems to imply something to do with moderating erratic or extreme awards or rectifying erroneous ones, it would usually be claimed to have more to do with establishing a common standard which applies to all the candidates or pupils assessed. The two factors which moderation seeks to regulate are differences between individual assessors, or groups of them, and differences that may occur within individual assessors (that is, inter-assessor variation and intra-assessor variation).

One common procedure is to lay down criteria and/or marking schemes in advance of anyone assessing any pupils. The scheme is then trialled on 'model' answers (sometimes on video or audio tape), with each assessor interpreting the scheme on the basis of his or her experience. The convenor (chief examiner) then obtains each assessor's awards and chairs a discussion on how these were arrived at, especially the ones at odds with the consensus. One outcome of such an 'agreement trial' is that assessors who continue to deviate are not used; another is that the criteria or work scheme is modified. In particular, vague criteria which often do not produce a consensus are discarded.

Intra-assessor variation is less amenable to detection or correction. It is commonly acknowledged to occur when an assessor deals with a large number of cases, leading to a change in perception of criteria or of pupils' work in relation to them. One procedure which is possible in mass examinations is to recycle a selection of scripts or projects through the same assessor. Of course, the scripts have to be unmarked or not identified as having already been assessed. In a class or a school, this kind of procedure would not be practicable. In any case, factors such as knowing a pupil personally and seeing him or her as a pupil in an ability band are much more likely to influence assessment (these are referred to as 'halo-effects').

Moderation can be carried out after an assessment has been made. It can be done on the basis of expert judgement, or on the statistics available from the population under review. In the former case, the expert needs a procedure either to scan the results of every pupil's assessments or of particular groups or selected individual cases. When teachers assess coursework projects, an outsider's view gained from close scrutiny of projects in many schools can moderate both halo-effects (such as awarding a better grade than the product warrants to pupils who impress by their willingness, or giving a lower grade to a pupil who 'could not have done this by themselves') and within-school effects. Even though teachers have criteria or guidelines, their interpretation in relation to grade standards cannot be aligned with those of teachers in other schools without some kind of linkage.

On occasions, the moderator's procedure may pick out groups such as schools entering pupils for an assessment for the first time. Or, if borderline cases are identified, these may be reviewed. Where whole-population moderation is not possible, randomly selected schools or individuals may be reviewed. Indeed, one procedure is to tell every assessor that 'they might be selected' for a random review.

The TGAT proposed the creation of a regional system for moderating which would involve teachers, that is, assessors, from each school meeting to review their group awards in relation to the criteria set out in the national tests or other forms of assessment. These proposals would have been expensive to staff and to administer, but more importantly, large amounts of teaching time would have been required. The position in late 1990 was that the tests for seven-year-olds would provide each teacher with common reference points for their own teacher assessments. As there will be so many disjunctions between the national assessments (that is, a limited subset of attainment targets or statements of attainment; different methods of appraisal; and differing relevance to school courses), the expectation that common standards will prevail seems over-optimistic even where teachers confer with others from schools in their locality.

Statistical moderation can take several guises, too. On the one hand, individual assessors with particular characteristics may be identified. This is done quite readily when a common sample of scripts or performances (on audio or video tape) are assessed. Thus, the relatively lenient or severe or inconsistent assessor can be picked out by reference to the consensus standard. On the other hand, the data may be used to change the awards made to a group, according to a model distribution or some other fixed scale point.

An example of statistical moderation in a large secondary school department shows that quite simple methods can have a use. When the four sets of marks from accumulated class assessments were compared with external examination results, there was almost zero correlation. The reason was quite evident when a scatter plot in different colours was done showing each teacher's aggregated marks against grades. One teacher clustered in one zone, another in a different zone, one bunched in the centre and the other spread across the whole area. Technically speaking, teacher effects confounded the relationship; this conclusion was based on the broad equivalence of external results over a period of years. As the high- and low-raters declined to alter their practices, a statistical adjustment was made to bring each person's distribution onto a common mean value and similar spread. Why bother? The reason is extremely important. Parents' and pupils' expectations were being inflated in one case and unduly depressed in another and some pupils were probably dropping the option at the end of the fourth year needlessly. Over a period of time, the teachers began to discriminate more effectively, their distributions became less bunched and more clearly related to criteria rather than arbitrary ideas about good or poor work. Later on, the whole school was moved onto the same basis because communication with parents on option choices was found to be improved

The assessment objective of moderation, clearly, is to increase the reliability of an evaluation of each pupil, to give fair and accurate assessments to all. Teachers involved in devising assessments and in moderation, especially when the basis is concerned, may acquire a better appreciation of the curriculum, other people's interpretation of criteria and the standards that can be achieved. So moderation can, in certain circumstances, be of some value to teachers as well as to pupils.

References

AINSCOW, M. and TWEDDLE, D. A. (1979). *Preventing Classroom Failure: An Objectives Approach*. Chichester: Wiley.

AINSCOW, M. and TWEDDLE, D. A. (1988). *Encouraging Classroom Success*. London: David Fulton.

ALLANSON, J. (1989). Quoted in *Education*, Vol. 174, No. 16.

AMERICAN PSYCHOLOGICAL ASSOCIATION (1985). *Standards for Educational and Psychological Testing*. Washington, DC: American Educational Research Association, American Psychological Association/National Council on Measurement in Education (chair, NOVICK, M. R.).

BARKER-LUNN, J. C. (1970). *Streaming in the Primary School*. Slough: NFER.

BARTRAM, D. (1985). The Automation of Psychological Procedures: Towards some Guidelines for Management and Operation. Paper presented at BPS Conference on the Management and Operation of Computer-based Testing Procedures, University College London.

BECHER, T. and MACLURE, S. (1979). *Accountability in Education*. Windsor: NFER.

BLACK, H. B. and DOCKRELL, W. B. (1980). *Diagnostic Assessment in Secondary Schools. A Teacher's Handbook*. Edinburgh: Scottish Council for Research in Education.

BLACK, H. B. and DOCKRELL, W. B. (1984). *Criterion Referenced Tests in the Classroom*. Edinburgh: Scottish Council for Research in Education.

BRITISH PSYCHOLOGICAL SOCIETY (1980). 'Technical recommendations for psychological tests', *Bulletin of the British Psychological Society*, 33, 161–4.

BRITISH PSYCHOLOGICAL SOCIETY (1984). 'Note on the computerisation of printed psychological tests and questionnaires', *Bulletin of the British Psychological Society*, 37.

BRUNER, J. S., GOODNOW, J. J. and AUSTIN, G. A. (1956). *A Study of Thinking*. New York: Wiley.

BULLOCK REPORT. GREAT BRITAIN. DEPARTMENT OF EDUCATION AND SCIENCE (1975). *A Language for Life: Report of a Committee of Enquiry*. London: HMSO.

CAMPBELL, D. T. and FISKE, D. W. (1959). 'Convergent and discriminant validation by the multitrait–multimethod matrix', *Psychological Bulletin*, 56.

CARROLL, B. B. and SAPON, S. M. (1955–59). *Modern Language Aptitude Tests*. New York: Psychological Corporation.

CHILD, D. (1970). *Essentials of Factor Analysis*. London: Holt, Rinehart and Winston.

CLOSS, S. J. (1980). *Job Ideas and Information Generator: Computer Assisted Learning*. Edinburgh: Hodder and Stoughton Educational.

COCKCROFT REPORT. GREAT BRITAIN. DEPARTMENT OF EDUCATION AND SCIENCE (1982). *Mathematics Counts: Report of a Committee of Enquiry*. London: HMSO.

CRONBACH, L. J. (1970). *Essentials of Psychological Testing* (3rd edn). New York: Harper and Row.

DENTON, C. and POSTLETHWAITE, N. (1985). *Able Children: Identifying them in the Classroom*. Windsor: NFER-NELSON.

DEPARTMENT OF EDUCATION AND SCIENCE AND WELSH OFFICE (1988). *English for Ages 5 to 11*. London: HMSO.

DEPARTMENT OF EDUCATION AND SCIENCE AND WELSH OFFICE (1988). *Mathematics for Ages 5 to 16*. London: HMSO.

DEPARTMENT OF EDUCATION AND SCIENCE AND WELSH OFFICE (1988). *National Curriculum, Design and Technology Working Group: Interim Report*. London: HMSO.

DEPARTMENT OF EDUCATION AND SCIENCE AND WELSH OFFICE (1988). *National Curriculum, Task Group on Assessment and Testing: A Report*. London: HMSO.

DEPARTMENT OF EDUCATION AND SCIENCE AND WELSH OFFICE (1988). *Science for Ages 5 to 16*. London: HMSO.

DEPARTMENT OF EDUCATION AND SCIENCE AND WELSH OFFICE (1981). *The Education (School Governing Bodies) Regulations*. London: HMSO.

DEPARTMENT OF EDUCATION AND SCIENCE AND WELSH OFFICE (1983). *The Education (Special Educational Needs) Regulations*. London: HMSO.

DEPARTMENT OF EDUCATION AND SCIENCE AND WELSH OFFICE (1984). *Records of Achievement: A Statement of Policy*, London.

DRIVER, R., GOTT, R., JOHNSON, S., WORSLEY, C. and WYLIE, F. (1982). *Science in Schools: Age 15. Report No. 1*. Assessment of Performance Unit Report. London: HMSO.

ELLIOTT, C. D., MURRAY, D. J. and PEARSON, L. S. (1983). *British Ability Scales* (2nd edn). Windsor: NFER-NELSON.

ENGEL-CLOUGH, E., DAVIES, P. and SUMNER, R. (1984). *Assessing Pupils: A Study of Policy and Practice*. Windsor: NFER-NELSON.

FOXMAN, D., RUDDOCK, G., JOFFE, L., MASON, K., MITCHELL, P. and SEXTON, B. (1985). *Mathematical Development: A Review of Monitoring in Mathematics 1978–1982* (Parts 1 and 2). London: DES.

FRY, E. B. (1968). 'A readability formula that saves time', *Journal of Reading*, 11.

GIPPS, C., STEADMAN, S., BLACKSTONE, T. and STIERER, B. (1983). *Testing Children*. London: Heinemann Educational Books.

GOLDSTEIN, H. (1985). Sex Bias and Test Norms in Educational Selection. Paper presented at BERA, Sheffield.

GRAY, J., JESSON, D. and JONES, B. (1984). 'Predicting differences in examination results between LEAs: does school organisation matter?', *Oxford Review of Education*, 10, 1, 45–68.

GUILFORD, J. P. (1965). *Fundamental Statistics in Psychology and Education* (4th edn). New York: McGraw-Hill.

HALSEY, P. (1989). Letter to Secretary of State for Education and Science from Chairman of School Examinations and Assessment Council, London.

HARGREAVES, D. (1986). 'Assessment and evaluation: a view from the ILEA.' In: *Assessment and Evaluation: Proceedings of the 1985 NFER Members' Conference*. Slough: NFER.

HARRIS, D. and BELL, C. (1986). *Evaluating and Assessing for Learning*. London: Kogan Page.

HART, K., BROWN, M., KUCHEMANN, D., KERSLAKE, D. and RUDDOCK, G. (1977–84). *Chelsea Diagnostic Mathematics Tests*. Windsor: NFER-NELSON.

HECKHAUSEN, N. (1967). *The Anatomy of Achievement Motivation*. New York: Academic Press.

HIERONYMOUS, A. N., LINDQUIST, E. F. and FRANCE, N. (1975). *Richmond Tests of Basic Skills*. Windsor: NFER-NELSON.

HOLLY, P. and SOUTHWORTH, G. (1989). *The Developing School*. Lewes: Falmer Press.

JESSON, D. (1988). 'School effectiveness and efficiency.' In *Quality in Schools: A Briefing Conference*. Slough: NFER.

JONES, G., CATO, V., HARGREAVES, M. and WHETTON, C. (1989). *Touchstones: Cross Curricular Group Assessments*. Windsor: NFER-NELSON.

KEYS, W. and FOXMAN, D. (1989). *A World of Differences: A United Kingdom Perspective on an International Assessment of Mathematics and Science*. Slough: NFER.

KYLES, I. and SUMNER, R. (1977). *Tests of Attainment in Mathematics in Schools: Continuation of Monitoring Feasibility Study*. Slough: NFER.

LAPOINTE, A. E., MEAD, N. A. and PHILLIPS, G. W. (1989). *A World of Differences: An International Assessment of Mathematics and Science*. Princeton, New Jersey: Educational Testing Service.

LEE, B. and DICKSON, P. (1989). *Assessment in Action*. Slough: NFER.

LEVY, P. and GOLDSTEIN, H. (1984). *Tests in Education: A Book of Critical Reviews*. London: Academic Press.

LEWIS, D. G. (1967). *Statistical Methods in Education*. London: University of London Press.

MCCALL, J. and BRYCE, T. (1982). Techniques for the Assessment of Practical Skills. Paper presented at Fifth International Symposium on Testing, Stirling University.

MCCLELLAND, D. C. (1961). *The Achieving Society*. New York: Van Nostrand.

MARKS, J., COX, C. and POMIAN-SRZEDNICKI, M. (1983). *Standards in English Schools*. London: National Council for Educational Studies.

MASLOW, A. H. (1954). *Motivation and Personality.* New York: Harper.

MILWARD, C. *et al.* (1973). *Yardsticks: Criterion Referenced Tests in Mathematics.* Windsor: NFER-NELSON.

MURPHY, P. (1988). 'TGAT: A conflict of purpose', *Curriculum*, 9, 3.

NASH, I. (1989). 'The civil servant with a lot of explaining to do', *Times Educational Supplement*, 26 May.

PAGE, R. and NASH, M. (1980). *Teenage Attitudes to Technology and Industry.* London: Standing Conference on Schools' Science and Technology.

PEACOCK, A. (1985). *Science Skills: Teach and Test.* Basingstoke: Macmillan Education.

QUALTER, A. (1988). 'Serving many purposes: aggregating scores – does it work?' *Curriculum*, 9, 3.

RIDGWAY, J. (1987). *A Review of Mathematics Tests.* Windsor: NFER-NELSON.

ROAT, J., WOLTER, F. de KLERK and VRIES de, MARC (1987). *Report of Pupils' Attitudes Towards Technology Conference.* Eindhoven: University of Technology.

ROSS, J. M. *et al.* (1972). *A Critical Appraisal of Comprehensive Education.* Slough: NFER.

RUSHTON, J. (1976). 'Personality and learning.' In: ROBERTS, T. (Ed) *The Circumstance of Learning.* Manchester: University of Manchester School of Education.

SHAYER, M., WYLAM, H., ADEY, P. and KUCHEMANN, D. (1979). *CSMS Science Reasoning Tasks.* Windsor: NFER.

SKURNIK, L. S., JEFFS, P. M. and KAWA, T. (Administrator's Manual compiled by NUTTALL, D.) (1971). *Science Attitudes Questionnaire.* Slough: NFER.

STERNBERG, R. J. (1985). *Beyond IQ.* Cambridge: Cambridge University Press.

STOTT, H. D. (1983). *Issues in the Intelligence Debate: A Juxtaposition of the Argument and an Appraisal.* Windsor: NFER-NELSON.

SUMNER, R. (1976). 'Motivation and achievement.' In: ROBERTS, T. (Ed) *The Circumstance of Learning.* Manchester: University of Manchester School of Education.

SUMNER, R. (1986). 'Selection.' In: YOUNGMAN, M. (Ed) *Midschooling Transfer.* Windsor: NFER-NELSON.

SUMNER, R. and BRADLEY, K. (1978). *Assessment for Transition.* Windsor: NFER.

SUMNER, R. and WARBURTON, F. W. (1972). *Achievement in Secondary School Attitudes, Personality and School Success.* Slough: NFER.

SWANN REPORT. GREAT BRITAIN. DEPARTMENT OF EDUCATION AND SCIENCE (1985). *Education for All: The Report of the Committee of Enquiry into the Education of Children from Ethnic Minority Groups.* London: HMSO.

TAYLOR REPORT. GREAT BRITAIN. DEPARTMENT OF EDUCATION AND SCIENCE (1977). *A New Partnership for Schools: Report of Committee of Enquiry.* London: HMSO.

VALLANCE, E. (1986). 'A second look at "Conflicting Conceptions of Curriculum" ', *Theory into Practice,* XXV, 1.

VERNON, P. E. (1971). *The Structure of Human Abilities.* London: Methuen.

VINCENT, D. and CRESSWELL, M. (1976). *Reading Tests in the Classroom.* Windsor: NFER-NELSON.

VINCENT, D. with POWNEY, J., GREEN, L. and FRANCIS, J. (1983). *A Review of Reading Tests.* Windsor: NFER-NELSON.

WARNOCK REPORT. GREAT BRITAIN. DEPARTMENT OF EDUCATION AND SCIENCE (1978). *Special Educational Needs: Report of a Committee of Enquiry into the Education of Handicapped Children and Young People.* London: HMSO.

WELTON, J., WEDELL, K. and VORHAUS, G. (1982). *Meeting Special Educational Needs: The 1981 Education Act and its Implications.* London: Heinemann Educational Books.

WRIGHT, B. D. and STONE, M. H. (1979). *Best Test Design: A Handbook for Rasch Measurement.* Chicago: University of Chicago/Social Research Inc.

Index

attainment
  factors influencing 42, 44
  levels 17, 28, 43
  list of 201
  predictors 52
  tests 17, 49–50, 51–2, 122–4, 177
  see also high ability, learning
  difficulties *and* special
  educational needs
attainment targets
  assessment 3, 4, 6, 7, 16, 156, 161
  national 16, 26, 145, 154, 158, 210
  profiles 18, 19, 210
  progress reports 158
  USA minimal competency 25
attitude scales 54–6
attributes measurement 38–42
audio tape use 216
automation extension 210–11, 214
average
  deviation 72–3
  group 94
  score 18, 99

banding of pupils 17, 31
Barker-Lunn, J. C. 55, 220
Bartram, D. 210, 220
battery of tests 58, 122
Becher, T. and Maclure, S. 19, 222
bi-variate distribution 129, 130,
  131–2, 134
Black, H. B. and Dockrell, W. B. 27,
  28, 222
borderline cases 217
British Ability Scales 43, 98
British Psychological Society 170,
  211
Bruner, J. S. *et al.* 49, 221
Bullock Committee 2, 18, 221

Campbell, D. T. and Fiske, D. W.
  166, 221
capability tests 62
careers guidance 32, 53
Carroll, B. B. and Sapon, S. 51–2, 221
categorical tests 63
centiles 80–1, 89
chain-back principle 168
Child, D. 140, 221

chi-square 125–8
City and Guilds syllabuses 23
classificatory tests 63
clerical tests 47
coaching 41
Cockcroft Report 2
cognitive functioning 49, 50
competence, minimal 25, 33
component levels 6
comprehensive education 200
computers
  administered tests 28, 53, 63, 179,
    210–12
  data analysis programs 100, 102,
    116, 130, 137, 139, 140, 160, 210,
    212
  educational guidance systems 32
  mathematics tests analysis 59
  network extension 210
  scoring systems 100, 210, 212
  test difficulties analysis 169
  use of by pupils 18
conceptual development 47–8, 49
confidence bands 114, 122–3
consensus 13, 216, 218
consistency, problem of 14, 15
construct validity 167
conveners 216
convergent tests 62
core subjects 3, 4, 26, 201, 207
correlational study 166
correlation coefficient 100, 119,
  120–1, 128–34, 136–7, 159–60
coursework projects 217
criterion referenced 57, 62, 64, 65,
  78, 124, 160–1, 215
criterion referenced validity 161
critical ration 116–17, 120, 185–7
Cronbach, L. J. 79, 221
curriculum
  changes 18
  evaluation 124–5
  improvement 32–3
  ordinary 124–8
  purpose of 171
  technology bases 124–8
Curriculum, National
  acceptance of 2